MOMENTOUS YEARS

Life and Times of a Teacher - Diplomat

LIM CHIN LEONG

Title
MY MOMENTOUS YEARS

Author
LIM CHIN LEONG

Copyright © 2020 Lim Chin Leong

First Published in 2021

Published by
Pen International Pte Ltd
80 Marine Parade Road
#09-08, Parkway Parade
Singapore 449269
info@penintl.com

ISBN : 978-981-18-0140-2

National Day Award (2014): Tribute to Lim Chin Leong as a
Pioneer of the Ministry of Foreign Affairs. A salute from
Mr K. Shanmugam, Minister for Foreign Affairs and Law.

LIM CHIN LEONG

CERTIFICATE-IN-EDUCATION (SINGAPORE T.T.C.)
BA HONS. (ENGLISH), UNIVERSITY OF LONDON
NATIONAL DAY AWARDS
PINGAT BAKTI SETIA (PBS)
PIONEER OF MINISTRY OF FOREIGN AFFAIRS

THE LONG SERVICE AWARD

The last of the original six awards created in 1962, the Pingat Bakti Setia rewarded public servants who had served 25 years continuously in the Government, statutory boards, fields of education or in government-owned companies, and who were of "irreproachable character". By the time the design of this medal was changed on Aug 2, 1996, thousands had been awarded.

*Mr Lim Chin Leong Receives Award Of
Pingat Bakti Setia (PBS) / Long Service Award
From Minister Of Foreign Affairs Prof. S. Jayakumar
On National Day 1993*

MFA colleagues in exotic attire during presentation of National Day Award Pingat Bakti Setia (PBS) August 1993.

Figure 3. Third Diplomatic Position

CONTENTS

Preface.. IX

Chapter 1: My Early Life 1

Chapter 2: My Education 7

Chapter 3: Man Proposes, God Disposes 17

Chapter 4: My Winding Road to Marriage.......................31

Chapter 5: Providential Change of Career 45

Chapter 6: First Diplomatic Posting in Tokyo..................49

Chapter 7: Second Diplomatic Posting in New Delhi 73

Chapter 8: My 3-Year Stint in MFA Headquarters 89

Chapter 9: Third Diplomatic Posting in London............................97

Chapter 10: Fourth Diplomatic Posting in Kuala Lumpur........ 119

Chapter 11: Final Stint in MFA Headquarters 167

Chapter 12: Fifth and Last Posting in Cairo 181

Chapter 13: My Reflections and Beliefs after Retirement.......... 201

About the Author.. 233

PREFACE

A candid and compelling memoir of one man's journey from World War 2 Malaya of the 1940s to his early years in pre-independent Singapore when he worked as an English teacher to his subsequent entry into the Ministry of Foreign Affairs (MFA) in 1968.

Lim Chin Leong's narrative documents his eventful tenure spanning 29 years in various foreign missions viz. Tokyo, New Delhi, London, Kuala Lumpur, Cairo, MFA Headquarters as Assistant Director i/c Malaysia & Brunei, joining President Wee Kim Wee's entourage in his state visit to Brunei in July 1992.

Those were defining times in the political evolution of Singapore and Malaysia. Often tense and turbulent, Lim recounts his extraordinary encounters with the now legendary icons like Lee Kuan Yew, Tunku Abdul Rahman, Devan Nair, Maurice Baker, S. R. Nathan, Mahathir Mohamad, Musa Hitam, Anwar Ibrahim and many more.

In a more insightful context, the author mines his spiritual sojourns that illuminated the various stages of his public and private life. These meditative segments of the book reveal Chin Leong's deepest levels of devotion about treasuring an intense and personal relationship with God.

*J*ethro March
Editor

CHAPTER 1
MY EARLY LIFE

As an octogenarian, I have the benefit of hindsight to reveal how I have evolved spiritually to the state of being a firm believer in divine providence. For the benefit of the reader, divine providence is defined as the beneficent care of God towards you, your family and your extended family.

In my early boyhood, my mother related to me interesting stories of filial piety. As a result, I began to understand the meaning of love, obedience and honouring my parents who were toiling day and night to bring up the family of eight.

One day, my mother brought me to a Chinese temple to pray. My mother believed in divine help and asked a monk how she could continue her daily devotions to the deity at the temple which was far away from our home. Moreover, she was busy day and night with her household chores as well as helping my industrious father in the shop. The monk advised her to set up an altar in the home. The family altar was installed at the corridor entrance high enough to place joss sticks and red candles. I recall a special occasion when

1

the altar appeared to be burnt during the night while we were all asleep. We noticed this event in the morning as a sign of the deity's presence in protecting us. Otherwise, a fire disaster would have been the consequence.

This comes to mind of another fire incident in the home. One evening, my father and I were trying to pour out kerosene from a big tin into a small container while our maid was holding a candlelight. She unwittingly held it too close to the kerosene which suddenly burst into flames near our feet. I saw my left foot burning. I felt my skin burning like a sheet of paper. Instinctively I tried to beat out the flame which was spreading towards the left knee. I rushed to a nearby room with a hanging curtain and used it to smother the flame. I then saw my father tearing off the maid's clothing which caught fire. My father's feet were also burnt. We were all taken to hospital for treatment and discharged after a couple of days. We were still suffering from pain. The poor maid suffered the most. My father engaged a herbalist who lived near our house. After a few weeks, my father and I recovered, but the maid passed away.

Behind my house, there ran a river where I learnt to swim in the shallow sandy part. Every now and again, I trod on little eels wriggling under my feet. I did not feel any fear. Sometimes I encountered a snake gliding across the river. I was in the midst of nature and enjoyed swimming naked. One afternoon, I ventured into the deep part. To my horror, when I could not feel the riverbed with my feet, I panicked. I instinctively shouted for help as I bobbed up and down in the moving water at the riverbank, swallowing water in gulps. Suddenly my feet touched sand. As I stood up, I cried and uttered repeatedly in Hokkien that I was going to die as I found my way to the wooden platform where my mother washed her clothes everyday. There was nobody around at the time. As I cried, I vomited water and felt a sense of relief. I recovered after a while and decided not to tell anyone about it. I loved the river too much and did not wish to be prevented from swimming again. I had developed a passion for swimming which eventually led me to enhance my technique gaining considerable confidence in the process. I tested myself by swimming against strong currents. With my clothes in one hand, I could swim across the river to and fro without mishap. I saved a classmate from drowning when he suddenly drifted into a deep part of the river.

One early morning, I walked to our latrine, a wooden shed which was situated adjacent to the river. As was my usual practice, I kept the door open. While I was defecating, I heard a loud splash. Earlier on, I had seen my immediate neighbour, a woman who was heavily pregnant washing on her wooden platform. Without hesitation, I rushed out in the nude and plunged into the water in her direction. She was already struggling in the water helplessly. Fortunately she was only a couple of feet away from the platform. I managed to lift her up and placed her on the platform with some considerable effort. She immediately called for her husband who came down running looking startled. They thanked me repeatedly as I swam back to my platform in order to get ready to go to school. When I returned from school, my parents told me joyfully that the couple next door expressed with gifts their eternal gratitude for having saved two lives!

Apart from swimming, I also took up kung fu which I learnt from my father and my uncle who was a professional kung fu master. My father installed a bag of sand in the backyard and encouraged me to practise punching on it to improve my reflexes and strengthen my hands. At the same time, I also studied 'dynamic tension' developed by a famous bodybuilder named Charles Atlas who taught the use of bicycle tubes, sticks or bricks to strengthen your hands, legs, pectoral muscles, abdominal muscles etc. Eventually I developed a strong body which was essential for kung fu. I felt confident that I was no longer a '7-stone weakling'. In the evening when I had no homework to do, I would sometimes go to the nearby cinema to watch a kung fu film. The kung fu films which I watched imbued me with a sense of heroism. Occasionally there were kung fu demonstrations at the roadside. Having observed their moves intently, I would return home to practise them earnestly as I desired to defend myself against bullies. Eventually I developed considerable confidence. My younger brothers were in the same school as myself. On one occasion, when I was told that my second brother was being manhandled by a big bully, I instantly rushed to confront him by grabbing his shirt collar and threatened to strike him with my strong arm. He was visibly shaken. Since that day, he became less aggressive when he learnt from somebody that I knew kung fu.

On another occasion, a certain prefect who intimidated me before was walking down the staircase staring at me as I walked up towards him. At the point of encounter, he deliberately tried to push me off. By applying the appropriate kung fu move, I managed to grasp his hand and pulled him tumbling down. The confrontation ended there and then.

A more serious confrontation between my father and his aggressive tenant was in the offing. The tenant had been stealing planks from the rented house. My father decided to evict him thereby making him furious. Late in the afternoon, he came with his detective friend to challenge my father to a fight outside the shop. I was present at the encounter. While my father was engaged in conversation with the detective, he threw a hard and direct punch at my father's face. My father fell down. I was enraged and pounced upon him from behind as he attempted to pull out his dagger from his trouser pocket. I instantly applied a stranglehold on his neck. As I strangled his neck harder, I heard him choking. As I had no intention of killing him, I released my grip and turned round to face him. In doing so, I struck his face with a few blows enough to make him groggy. I could also see his nose bleeding. He ran off leaving his friend in the lurch. Immediately I advanced towards him with a fierce mien. I warned him that I could report him to the Chief Police Officer whose son was my classmate and friend. I told him in no uncertain terms to bring the culprit to seek pardon from my father whose nose bled as a result of that sudden punch. Later in the evening, the detective brought the culprit to my father to apologise and seek pardon for his misdeeds. A year later, I heard from my parents that he was hanged for murder.

Born in Kluang, Johor. Educated in Govt English School (Now Sekolah Tinggi Kluang). Lower pic shows the bridge & river where author swam naked!

CHAPTER 2
MY EDUCATION

As a businessman, my father came in contact with different kinds of successful people from whom he could seek advice and help. He had very limited education, because my migrant grandfather from China was an opium smoker who earned his income by being a barber. He expected my father to fend for himself. No wonder he began his career as a professional barber. He saved money by giving us quick and neat haircuts. As time passed by, he earned enough money to start a bicycle repairing business in addition to his barber's trade. My mother was a great help to him.

Realising the importance of education for the sake of my future, my father sent me to a Chinese school to learn Mandarin at the tender of five. After a year, he got me admitted into a private English school, believing it was a better option as Malaya then was ruled by the British.

In December 1941, the Japanese attacked Malaya. I was still very young. I recall myself and my parents running out of the house to hide ourselves among the lalang and bushes at the back as the Japanese aeroplanes flew overhead dropping bombs. By divine providence, I could see the bombs exploding in mid-air as they flew across the town. One afternoon, while I was sitting on the chair at the five-foot path of my house, I saw a column of Japanese infantry soldiers marching along Mersing Road in front of my house towards the town bridge nearby. My immediate neighbour on the right shouted in Hokkien to me, *"Don't you know death!"* Indeed the whole row of shop houses had their doors closed except mine. My parents were at the rear of the house which had a long corridor. They did not know that I was outside the house. How clueless I was then as a small boy.

During the Japanese Occupation, my father was forced to send me to a Japanese school where I learnt how to speak and write Japanese as well as strict discipline. As far as my father was concerned, I proved to be useful to him as the Japanese soldiers patronised his bicycle shop and he made use of me as an interpreter. On one occasion which I recall distinctly, a Japanese soldier drove his truck to seek my father's assistance in locating a particular address. My father called out to me for help. As I approached the soldier, he asked me thus, *"Kodomo (boy), can you speak Japanese?"* I said yes. He appeared pleased and gave me a kindly smile. We found the location quickly and he drove me back to the shop. He uttered *'arigato'* to me and I bade him *'sayonara'* with a bow. Quite surprisingly, the next day his subordinate delivered a sack of rice which we appreciated very much as it was a scarce commodity in those days.

Sometime in August 1945, a momentous event took place. A large number of Chinese including my father were rounded up and hauled by trucks to the town padang. The talk of the town was that they would be massacred for suspected treason. We prayed fervently to God for divine intervention. As the machine guns were on the ready, a message came from the Japanese military headquarters ordering a halt to the planned execution. How amazing! We were tremendously relieved. This is really divine providence. Incidentally, decades later I was destined by divine providence to be sent to Tokyo to help set up the thirteenth Singapore Embassy on the 32nd floor of the first earthquake-proof building, earning the reputation of being the "highest Embassy in Tokyo".

After the surrender of Japan in 1945, the British returned to Malaya. I saw a number of British officers patronising shops using their own currency. There was a shortage of paper currency. We were told to use stamps to pay for goods such as stationery, groceries etc. I recall using stamps valued at 1/4, 1/2 and 1 cent to buy ice cream and sweets. However, where bread was concerned, there was a shortage and many buyers, including a young boy like me, had to elbow their way to the door barrier and stretch their hands with the correct sum of money to get a hot loaf of nice smelling bread from the shopkeeper!

Realising the importance and usefulness of the English language, my father tried to get me admitted into the only Government English School in Kluang, Johor where I was born. He was not successful. The school clerk, who knew my father whom he addressed in Malay as 'gemuk' (stout), advised him to try again. My father humbly implored him for help. In the meantime, he advised my father to place me in Jubilee School (a private English school). He promised to help. Before the school year ended, he rode on his bicycle to tell my father that there was a vacancy for me. One day, my father took me to see the headmaster. After the interview which was conducted in English, we received the good news that I had been admitted into the primary school. From then on, I studied diligently and won book prizes every year.

The teachers appointed me as Assistant Librarian, Assistant Editor of the school magazine, Vice-Chairman of the school debating society, mass drill leader as well as encouraged me to participate in oratorical contests and act in a play such as "Robin Hood and his Merry Men". I acted as Friar Tuck (a rotund figure) and stepped on a banana skin causing me to tumble backwards. The audience laughed their heads off! As time passed by, I developed fluency in my speech and a love for words (logophile). I read voraciously Greek and Roman mythologies. I scored high marks in my English examinations. My English teacher, Mr A.C. Lewis, a Catholic with 12 children, personally rewarded me with a copy of 'CHAMBERS 20th CENTURY DICTIONARY'. I used the dictionary very often for doing crossword puzzles and earned a few prizes awarded by the Straits Times. I also enjoyed reading a particular history book entitled "A History of the British Empire". There were many bombastic words in that book and I delighted in learning them. Every now and then, I would bombard my classmates with those words. My classmates found the history lessons boring whereas I enjoyed listening to the teacher who was helpful and kind to me. As a result, I developed a great interest in history until today. I also obtained a grade A in history for my Senior Cambridge Certificate.

For my second language, I studied Mandarin taught by a beautiful Shanghai lady teacher who spoke with a 'musical' accent. I found Mandarin more difficult than English because of its tones, number of strokes to remember in a traditional Chinese character, varied meanings in the same character and a lot of compulsory recitations by heart.

When I was in standard VIII, a year before my Senior Cambridge Exams, a Malay teacher approached me and persuaded me to take up Malay in his new class which he was preparing for the Senior Cambridge Malay examination. I consulted my father who advised me to do Malay as the country was going to be in the hands of the Malays sooner or later. I then switched to Malay which I found to be easy. Translation of Malay passages into English and vice versa was compulsory, which was easy for me but quite difficult for my Malay classmates. In the end, I was the only Chinese candidate who scored a credit while a few Malay candidates passed. My Malay teacher was extremely pleased with my performance. I did him proud.

My headmaster Charles Donald Westwood had the greatest influence on me. He was very encouraging and paid special attention to my needs. Whenever he saw me in the afternoon doing my extra-curricular activities, he would beckon me over and asked me thus, *"How are you, son?"* I would reply, *"I am all right, sir"* in a shy manner. Sometimes he would rub my hair and inquired, *"Do you need money?"* He knew that my father usually gave me a small pittance. With a smile, he would ask, *"How much do you need? Five dollars?"* As a Chinese brought up in the traditional custom, I should decline the offer. So I said, *"No need, sir."* He continued insistently, *"No, you are not being honest with me."* When he uttered this, I plucked up courage and responded, *"Two dollars will do, sir."* He reacted in a fatherly manner with the following words, *"That's my boy!"* Pleased with my response, he instantly took out his worn-out leather wallet and pressed a $5 note in my hand. He probably perceived me as a good all-round student who deserved to be helped. One afternoon, I was quite surprised when he drove to my house to meet my parents. I was as usual swimming in the river behind. My mother shouted for me, telling me that my headmaster was in the house. Luckily I was in my swimming trunks when I finally appeared in his presence.

He looked at me intently. I felt embarrassed and after a brief conversation, he departed. Since that time, he would invite me to have dinner together with Mahmood, who was from Muar and the head prefect of my school, lodging with him. Years later, Mahmood became a district officer of Muar.

My ambition in that period was to be a doctor in order to save lives. Where my parents were concerned, they would fall ill due to long hours of work and insufficient rest or sleep, especially my mother. They would consult a TCM physician rather than a western-trained doctor because it was cheaper. One incident particularly angered me when I brought my mother to see a western-trained doctor. He was not kind and refused the injection which my mother pleaded with him to give. There were many other sick people who just could not afford to pay the medical fees. So they were left to their own devices. All these circumstances made me resolve to be a doctor.

However, my father promised to see me through my education up to Senior Cambridge only. He said that if I wanted to go for higher studies, I would have to find other means on my own. The name Westwood came to my mind but by then, I heard that he had been promoted as Director of Education for the state of Johor after he received the award of 'Member of the British Empire'. He was then transferred to Johor Bahru. I plucked up courage to write a letter to him. He sent me a quick reply and offered to pay the university fees if I agreed to study for a BA degree. He revealed that he was already committed to supporting a student in Australia. Therefore, it was beyond his means to send me for medical studies. As my father could not decide for me, I approached my aunt who was a rice merchant for financial support. She appreciated my ambition and agreed to help. The other problem I encountered was accommodation in Singapore.

A good Malay classmate offered to ask his uncle named Hussein, a meteorological officer, to accommodate me in Singapore. He put in a good word for me with the result that he would only charge $30 per month. I was prepared to sleep with a mat on the floor if there was no room in the government quarters. Hussein recommended that I seek admission to St Andrew's School which was located not far from his home. With his help, I was admitted into the HSC class doing Biology, Chemistry, Physics and General Paper. That was the first time I mixed with many Jewish students. The principal was Francis Thomas, an Anglican who occasionally lectured to us. Another teacher whom I remember was Canon Adam who conducted chapel service in the school. I was invited to join them for prayers. The school would celebrate special occasions in the St Andrew's Cathedral.

Four months into my studies, I received a message that my aunt had died of diabetes. I was informed that her children needed funds for further studies. I took the news in my stride and planned with silent prayers to the Lord to change the course of my life. First, I approached P.S.Raman who taught us General Paper. He kindly offered to check whether I was eligible for a government scholarship. According to him, I was well qualified under 'academic qualifications'. When he inquired of my nationality, I disclosed that I was a Johor national. He regretted to inform me that I was ineligible for the scholarship. That ended my hope. Nevertheless, I remember him for his kindness. Surprisingly, many years later, our paths crossed again when he was appointed as our Ambassador to Moscow while I was undergoing training as a foreign service officer, having been seconded from the Ministry of Education. Very much later, I also worked with his son Bilahari Kausikan, who was the Director of

Southeast Asia Division while I was the Assistant Director for Malaysia and Brunei.

Amazingly, soon after my failure to secure the scholarship, there appeared an advertisement in The Straits Times inviting applications for admission to the Singapore Teachers Training College. I immediately applied and in due time, I was called for interview. The selection board found me suitable for the two-year Certificate-in-Education course. I was told by the Bursar that I would be paid an allowance of $100 per month. I was overjoyed because it was enough to cover the cost of my lodging and saved my parents from having to send a subsistence allowance of $30 per month. As for transport, I depended on my Raleigh bicycle which my father gave to me as a reward for having achieved Grade I Senior Cambridge Certificate in 1954.

In 1955, I attended the Teachers Training College and graduated in 1957. I recollect my active participation in my studies as well as sports in which I excelled, especially in swimming and athletics. My activities were recorded in the College magazine. I also took part in oratorical contests. Then there came a far more challenging contest. One of my seniors encouraged me to challenge Harry Elias for the post of President of the Students' Union. It was a close fight, losing by a narrow margin to Harry. It was all in good fun and we celebrated the occasion with a dinner and dance. Harry Elias is today a legal eagle with his own firm while I ended up as a pioneer of the Ministry of Foreign Affairs.

New Straits Times 19-3-1991 mentioned Mr Lim taught for
10 yrs before joining foreign service. This is his professional
teaching Certificate in Education.

CHAPTER 3
MAN PROPOSES,
GOD DISPOSES

I have chosen the above well-known proverb from the Bible, the most widely-read book in the world. We make plans but it is God who decides whether our plans will be realised. It is very true indeed, judging by my own experiences. I will reveal them as my narrative of events unfold.

I recall two prophetic statements my father made to me before my departure by train to Singapore. One was that I would fare better in a big city. The other was that besides English, I should keep up my Malay studies. I took his advice seriously.

In Singapore, unlike my hometown Kluang, there were far more facilities and amenities which I could avail myself of. Kluang in Malay means 'flying fox'. The beauty of the town lies in two adjoining mountains in the shape of a flying fox. As a curious teenager, I ventured, without telling my parents, to climb the mountain slope. I realised later on that climbing up the steep slope was less risky than descending it. By the grace of God, I did not come to grief.

When I left in 1955, there were growing shouts of 'Merdeka!' in the town centre. When I arrived in Singapore to attend the Teachers Training College, the atmosphere was different. The political situation was well controlled by the colonial government. I was able to complete my training as a qualified teacher in 1957. I felt elated being paid a salary of $475 per month. This enabled me to buy a small second-hand car. On one of my rare trips back from Kluang to Singapore, I was stopped at a roadblock by a policeman who asked whether I carried any prohibited material such as paper. I was taken aback and felt a little nervous. He looked me in the eyes. With a smile, I declared in Malay that I had some writing paper in my briefcase. He remarked that under emergency regulations, I should be detained for interrogation. That frightened me and instantly I pleaded with him by revealing that I was a teacher in Singapore and was truly sorry for not being aware of the emergency regulations. Thereupon, he let me off. I felt great relief and thanked him in Malay for his compassion (belas kasihan). As I drove off, I expressed my eternal gratitude to God.

My first posting was to Bukit Panjang Government Secondary School where I was requested to set up a science laboratory to teach the lower secondary students in General Science. After a year, I was transferred to Gan Eng Seng Chinese Middle School to teach English as a second language. Before long, I was again transferred to Thomson Chinese Middle School to teach English. Here I taught upper middle class students until 1962. I was earnest in improving their standard of English. I could see their great interest in wanting to speak and write good English. It was a joy to teach them. I would spend hours correcting their books until 7.00pm when I would leave the school for dinner. Sometimes the principal Chen See How, a well-known personality in the Teochew community, would urge me to go home. I would respond with a smile, telling him that it did not bother me as I was a bachelor. The principal perceived me as a very responsible teacher and appointed me to take charge of the extra-curricular activities of the students. I noticed that some of the students would stay on until late in the evening. To find out whether they were influenced by communist ideology, I asked the students in class this question: *"Do you all believe in God?"* They exclaimed, *"No!"* I was not surprised, because I knew about communist insurgency in Malaya and heard of communist cells in certain schools in Singapore.

During this period of my life, I was surprised when a certain manager from Malaya Publishing House approached me one afternoon trying to persuade me to write a series of English textbooks to replace those that I was using to teach the upper secondary students. I was reluctant initially but as our discussion went on, I eventually agreed. His comment was that the English books contained many foreign materials which the Chinese students could not appreciate. That was also my observation.

Following this event, Patrick Hernon, an Englishman teaching English in Raffles Institution, turned up one morning to observe my method of teaching English as a second language. He was impressed and thanked my principal for permission to observe me in class. He also introduced his charming Chinese wife named Rosie who spoke Mandarin and English fluently.

There was a Hong Kong lady teacher teaching Mandarin by the name of Maria Tzu. She could speak English though not fluently. When she knew that I was going to write an English textbook, she suggested visiting her friend Dr Han Suyin in Johor Bahru, whose name I recognise as a renowned author, especially through her famous novel about love entitled "A Many-Splendoured Thing". I recollect that Maria Tzu's name was also mentioned in that novel. We arrived at her blue-painted house. She was waiting for us at the doorway and Maria introduced me as a school colleague who was approached to write an English textbook for Chinese students. She was friendly and came across as a slender and tanned lady in a cheongsam. I had earlier on gathered that she was a Chinese-born Eurasian physician lecturing in Nanyang University in Singapore.

Before settling down for tea, she introduced her partner, an Indian Army officer named Joseph, who sat quietly in a corner listening to our confab. Dr Han suggested that I approach Leon Comber, a Singapore publisher, for assistance. She was in a garrulous mood so much so that Maria and I could hardly chip in. After an hour or so, I decided to leave. As we walked out, I noticed two other similar houses as hers built in a row. I inquired, pointing to the blue houses, *"Whose are those?"* Instantly she answered tersely, *"Mine."* As I drove off towards Singapore, I began to muse on the need to approach Leon Comber. In the end, I decided not to do so.

For the next three months, I spent my spare time typing my draft copy of the English textbook using all my teaching materials as well as incorporating excerpts from the books of a few famous authors and a speech by Prime Minister Lee Kuan Yew concerning the education of our youth. Some time was also required to seek permission from the authors and publishers. Amazingly, a former teacher of St Andrew's School by the name of Cheong Hock Hai sent me a memo requesting an interview with him in his position as the Ministry of Education's Adviser on School Textbooks. During the interview, he told me that MPH had sent him the final draft copy of my textbook entitled "A Book of

Comprehension, Precis and Composition Exercises for Secondary English and Vernacular Schools." He asked me whether I could produce a series. I explained that I could not spare the time and further elaborated on how I had organised and graded the passages in the book according to difficulty in terms of language. The questions were framed in such a way as to encourage repetition of sentence structures in the student's answers. With a nod of his head, he approved it for publication. MPH later informed me that it would proceed to print 5000 copies for the first edition of the book. 4 copies were required by law to be deposited with the National Library. Amazingly, when I was again transferred to Queensway Secondary School, I learnt rather indirectly that my book was a recommended textbook for English Secondary Schools. A lady teacher approached me and inquired whether the book with the name Lim Chin Leong was written by me. I smiled and said delightedly, "Yes. In fact, I had produced the book for the benefit of my Chinese students in Thomson Chinese Middle School." Furthermore, I used it to teach adult students in the Adult Education Classes in the evenings. One afternoon when I went for Civil Defence Training, I met a teacher who was teaching in a Chinese school. During the course of our conversation, he asked for my name. When I mentioned my name, it rang a bell. He inquired whether I had written an English textbook. I nodded my head and said "yes". He told me that he was teaching English in his school and was using my textbook. He commented that it was a very helpful book.

Pirated editions of my book were later found in Bras Basah Road bookshops as well as in Johor. My youngest brother, who got a Johor state scholarship to do medicine in Singapore, wrote to me in Tokyo whether I wanted to sue them. I replied that I was not avaricious and that the purpose was to help students and adults to read and write

FOR STUDENTS IN CHINESE, MALAY AND TAMIL UPPER
SECONDARY SCHOOLS AND ENGLISH SECONDARY SCHOOLS

A Book of

Comprehension, Precis

and

Composition Exercises

LIM CHIN LEONG

M.P.H. PUBLICATIONS SDN. BHD. SINGAPORE

This was the first book by Mr Lim,
"A Book of Comprehension, Precis and Composition Exercises",
which was recommended by the Ministry of Education for
Vernacular and English secondary schools.

good English. Even MPH was not honouring its written agreement with me. As I was busy in Tokyo helping to set up the Singapore Embassy, I left the matter as it was, quoting the well-known proverb: *"Live and let live"*.

Another interesting event that occurred in the course of my teaching career in Queensway Secondary School was the opportunity to meet an attractive lady named Margaret Tan who was teaching the lower secondary classes. We were mutually attracted after our encounter at the school staircase. There was nobody around. Our brief conversation which was quite stimulating went like this: *"I notice you are fond of wearing white clothes. Your pants are rather broad."* To that comment came my immediate repartee, *"Wait till you see me in the buff!"* followed by bursts of laughter. She felt abashed and dashed off.

I was not aware then that she had a couple of admirers who were interested in her. One of them told me not to get too close to her in a jocular manner but his countenance showed otherwise. Nevertheless, we continued our relationship. On another occasion I heard that Margaret and her companions were going to watch a movie at Cathay cinema. I quietly trailed them and bought a first- class ticket without their knowledge. The next day I revealed to her that I saw her with her friends at the cinema. Her immediate reaction was: *"Why didn't you join us?"* I responded that I was not invited and added that a particular friend of hers might not be happy with me around. She remarked somewhat annoyed: *"That's none of his business."* I was delighted to hear her response.

Sometime later, I was instructed by the principal to attend a science course with the view to starting a Cambridge School Certificate class in General Science. I had already been trained as a science teacher for lower secondary classes. When the principal indicated from the Ministry's circular that I would earn two increments if I passed the course, I was naturally overjoyed as it meant additional income. I passed the course quite easily. Laus Deo! (Latin for Praise the Lord!) With increased income, I was able to afford better accommodation and moved to Stevens Guest House at 80, Stevens Road in District 9. I counted this as a blessing from God. All along, I had been staying in rented rooms, living with a Malay family at Arthur Road in Katong, an Indian family at Dunearn Road near Newton circus and a Chinese family at Cuff Road in Little India. I led a tranquil life with them except for one incident which I can still recall vividly. The Indian couple were kind to me and the wife was a very good cook. I loved her delicious mutton curry. Her husband Raju taught me Tamil so much so that it affected my English pronunciation. My English lady lecturer in observing me teaching poetry was surprised to note my Indian accent in reading this famous poem "The Rainbow" by William Wordsworth:-

> "My heart leaps up when I behold
> A rainbow in the sky:
> So was it when my life began;
> So is it now I am a man;
> So be it when I shall grow old,
> Or let me die!
> The Child is father of the Man;
> I could wish my days to be
> Bound each to each by natural piety."

By divine providence, the government posted me to London in 1977. That gave me and my family the opportunity to explore by car the Lake District where Wordsworth was born. He was one of the great British Romantic poets I had to study for my University of London B.A.Hons (English). He was appointed poet laureate in 1843.

Mr Lim's favourite poem "Rainbow" by Wordsworth. Explored his Lake District and cottage in August 1979. Windermere, Lake District, August 1979.

To Wordsworth's cottage on foot; serene atmosphere.
Grasmere, Lake District August 1979.

Beautiful landscapes in Lake District - England.

In his normal state, Raju appeared to be sober and well-behaved. It seemed to me that he had a nagging problem with his brother-in-law. One evening, both of them quarrelled loudly in the kitchen area. It attracted my attention. When I walked out of my room, I saw Raju being threatened with a knife. His wife tried to separate them but in vain. I shouted at them to stop the altercation. Out of respect for me, they halted. I beckoned Raju over to calm him down. However, this bitter problem rankled with him long after. He would from time to time take it out on his poor wife whenever he was drunk. She was docile and would just grin and bear it. It came to such a stage that I myself was adversely affected. He probably perceived me to be siding with his wife. One night, in his intoxicated state, he barged into my room to assault me. I managed to apply a judo lock on his neck. He was suffocating. Before I released him, I made him swear that he would not attack his pitiable wife who appeared emaciated. He suddenly yelled at me to get out. Quietly I left the room to hide myself in a nearby atap shed, where I met a demented man who agreed to put me up for the night. The next day when Raju was out at work, I went to collect my cast-out belongings and departed for my friend's house at Cuff Road in Little India.

In all the above homes where I stayed, I slept without a bed except in Stevens Guest House. One morning, as I lazed on my bed, I began to muse on the need for a 'permanent roof over my head'. That spurred me on to do a search for a suitable and affordable house. By divine providence, I drove into a new housing estate called Hongkong Park in Bukit Timah developed by Yat Yuen Hong Co. I contacted the manager who was kind enough to show me a list of prices. I chose the cheapest one at $18,000. After viewing the house with him, we returned to his office. By that time, it was already sold to someone. He advised me to take the next one at $21,000. As the difference in price was small, I decided there and then to buy it. I took altogether two mortgage loans from the developer and Malaya Borneo Building Society Ltd. They were to be repaid over a period of 15 years. I remember that my monthly salary was more than enough to cover the total cost of monthly instalments. By the grace of God, a certain agent, who had dealings with the British Army, approached me while I was inspecting the house and offered to rent it out for me. As the rent was more than the sum of my total monthly repayments, I accepted his offer. That was a great relief to me and I continued lodging happily in Stevens Guest House.

When I was staying in Stevens Guest House, I and Margaret quietly continued our courtship. We enjoyed our romantic rendezvous. One Saturday night, I drove her to Changi Beach to enjoy the sea breeze and amuse ourselves. Suddenly there appeared four young men emerging from a secluded spot, advancing towards my car. The gang leader knocked at my window, signalling to me to get out of my car. I did as he demanded. As a kung fu man, I tried to appear dauntless and positioned myself with my back facing my car. I heard the leader asking his men in Malay: *"Mau hantam dia?" (i.e. "Want to beat him up?")*. Instantly I took out my wallet and gave the money to the man next to me, saying to the leader: *"I have given all my money. There's no need to hantam me."* I could sense the leader was wary of me. His men remained silent. By divine providence, there was no fight and they walked away. Remember the proverb: *'Discretion is the better part of valour.'*

I also recall my kung fu master's sound advice: *'Those who live by the sword shall die by the sword.'*

CHAPTER 4
MY WINDING ROAD TO MARRIAGE

I did not have a girlfriend until I was 16 years old. My school was coeducational and I befriended this girl called Alice. She came from Malacca to live with her father who was the headmaster of a private Chinese school in Kluang. Her home was quite far from the school. I did not tell my parents of our relationship until one day she decided to move house with permission from her father. My parents initially did not object to renting a room to her. As time passed by, my stellar academic performance was adversely affected by my relationship with her, thereby causing serious concern to my parents.

Incidentally, I usually spent my school holidays in Malacca which was my favourite destination, even before meeting Alice. Eventually, my parents asked her to move out. As a filial son, I did not remonstrate with my parents, as they meant well. Moreover, at the back of my mind, there was this fixation to achieve my ambition to be a doctor. Thereafter, I did not keep up the relationship with her and it finally died away.

When I left for Singapore in 1955 to do my Cambridge H.S.C. in St Andrew's School, also a coeducational school, I did not get infatuated with, nor fall in love with any of the girls there. I had a close friend in school named Albert Goh whose father owned a big car. During weekends, he would invite me and his friends including female company to house parties and dances in his father's club. That was where I learnt how to dance and enjoyed it tremendously. There were many other activities which kept me occupied, as a result of which I never felt homesick. I had my faithful 'iron horse' (Raleigh bicycle) to transport me to my destinations.

After the death of my kind aunt, my life like a river meandered into a different field of education, i.e. teaching. I was then 19 years old and still living like a nomad. Everyday my iron horse would carry me from Katong to Cairnhill where the Teachers Training College was temporarily housed until it moved to Paterson Hill. I still cherish fond memories of my association with my expatriate and local lecturers.

One would have thought that I would find a lifetime companion in this College environment. Curiously enough, in one of my social outings, I came across a charming young lady with a sweet smile. I struck up a conversation with her. Towards the end of our confab, I asked whether I might one pay her a visit to her home. She answered readily and gave me her address and telephone number. Little did I realise that she intended to introduce her elder sister named Mabel. One day, after my meeting with her and Mabel, I began to muse: *"Was their family of 'Peranakan' descent? Was Mabel's sister asked by her parents to observe the custom?"* Despite the fact that I was never brought up with this Peranakan culture, I decided to give it a try and began to date Mabel, who was not as pretty as her younger sister. However, she was mild, spoke good English and worked in

32

A.I.A. Insurance headquarters at Robinson Road. We would meet at various rendezvous, e.g. Rendezvous Restaurant at Bras Basah Road, Botanical Gardens, Katong Park, Changi Beach and at the car park nearby the old Kallang Airport where we had our intimate moments together. I was then in the final year of my teacher's training course. I passed and persuaded her to attend my graduation ceremony, but as she was very shy, she begged to be excused and instead suggested that we meet in the evening at Katong Park. I was happy and met her at our rendezvous. Thereupon I took her to Katong Hotel where there was a night club. We had a special table to ourselves and relished our sumptuous dinner in the dim light. I asked whether she was game for a dance. Bashfully, she replied that she did not know how to dance. I offered to teach her the slow waltz and after some persuasion, she agreed. Since she had never danced before, she gave up after a few awkward attempts to avoid embarrassment. Since then, we never danced at all.

One day, I was introduced to her parents at her home. While her father was friendly and welcoming, her mother came across as a domineering matriarch, which made me feel uncomfortable. I could sense Mabel's nervousness. My reaction towards her mother was negative, which seemed to portend an unhappy relationship with her. I recall vividly an occasion when I was invited by Mabel's father to dine with the family at home. Her mother made a few patronising and offensive remarks during the dinner, which upset me, caus-ing me to quit the dinner and leave the house immediately. The next night, Mabel rang me up, apologising profusely and crying at the same time. It was heartbreaking to hear her sobs. Finally, I assured her that I would reconcile with her mother although not so soon.

Some time afterwards, Mabel telephoned me one after-noon whispering that her mother hoped I would agree to go with her to a particular jewellery shop to buy an engage-ment ring. Sensing a change of heart, I consented. We met at the designated jewellery shop where her mother selected a diamond ring. She assured me that she had got the best deal for me and it was the cheapest diamond ring in the showcase. I believed her and paid readily for it. Thereafter, to avoid any tiff with her, I would meet Mabel outside.

Everything seemed to be proceeding smoothly until one fateful evening. Mabel's parents had organised the celebra-tion of our engagement at their home. It was a Saturday. Mabel and I met in the afternoon and we decided to go to Changi Beach for a swim. Before that, she revealed to me that I stay with her in her house after marriage. All along, I was under the impression that she, as my wife, would be prepared to live with me and not with her parents. As there was no mutual consultation on this issue, I took it upon my-self to rent a large room in Little India as marriage was in the offing. At the time, I was putting up with my teacher-friend at Cuff Road in Little India. I was, of course, disappointed, mainly because I doubted whether I would ever be happy staying with her mother around.

Mabel pleaded with me to stay in her house. Nonetheless, I went along with her. Meanwhile, we had a dip in the waters until evening fell, when it was time for Mabel to take a taxi home. I was still in a reluctant mood and told her to go ahead while I lay on the beach, mulling over the issue. Suddenly I heard a voice in my head telling me not to attend the engagement party. So I lingered there until 11.00pm. When I finally reached home, my friend and his mother informed me that there were several phone calls asking for me. I expressed my thanks and apologies for having caused unnecessary disturbance to them. As expected, Mabel called me up the next morning and asked me to turn up at the office of The Straits Times to dissolve our engagement. I did as I was told with my close friend who was also a teacher. She returned my diamond ring. There and then, we parted for ever.

Following the above event, instead of grieving over the incident, I decided to move on in life and live in a new environment. That was how I came to stay in Stevens Guest House where I slept on a bed for the first time. Moreover, it was much nearer to the Thomson Chinese Middle School where I was posted to teach English. It was the most productive period of my life. By divine providence, it was here that I produced a useful English textbook for English and vernacular schools. Even today, I have fond memories of this place - particularly the kind and helpful manager, Mr Low; the obese and friendly English lady with her cute little boy; and the portly veteran lawyer from Sri Lanka (Ceylon), Mr Stoner Kadirgamar, who later moved out to another residence near his office but often kept in touch with me, because he was living alone in Singapore. At one time, I thought of taking up law because it was a more challenging profession, having observed Mr Stoner and Mr David Marshall arguing in court. They piqued my interest in law so much so that years later, as a diplomat, I became a student of Gray's Inn in London. But I could not complete my legal training due to my interrupted posting to Malaysia.

I remember vividly one incident in which David Marshall in his bush jacket got out of his car and yelled at a British Military Police who was trying to slap an Indian boy. He shouted very loudly: *"Don't you touch the boy, or else I will have you fixed!"* A crowd gathered to witness the scene. Thereupon he ceased, returned to his military jeep and drove off. I felt the force of his commanding voice. One day, Stoner took me to a Malayan court in Johor Bahru to see him in action. When the English judge saw me, he asked Stoner: *"Who is that gentleman sitting next to you?"* With a smile, he replied: *"He is my intern who is learning litigation. I hope your Honour will permit him to remain."* He nodded his approval and proceeded with the court case.

Apart from the above activities, I also spent my time during weekdays giving private tuition. I taught students who were weak in English and Mathematics in their homes, usually in the afternoon and sometimes in the evening. Their fathers were mainly businessmen. I never advertised but they knew me by word of mouth. All of them passed their weak subjects except for one who failed his Maths by a few marks. He was the son of a civil servant. He blamed his son for not studying hard. I assured the father of my confidence that he would pass his Maths in his second attempt. He took my word for it and asked me to continue teaching him Maths. The outcome, as expected, was that he scored good marks in his final examination, much to the joy of his parents and myself.

At this juncture, I would like to record two reminiscences. One evening, I had my chicken rice at a shop near my private students' residence. After my dinner, I was shocked to find my wallet missing. With a feeling of embarrassment, I approached the stallholder and told him the truth. I offered to leave my watch with him, assuring him that I would return the next day to hand him the money owed.

He looked at me, smiling and said, even though he did not know me: *"Don't worry. It's a small matter. No need to give me the watch. I trust you. Pay me anytime. You are welcome."* I was much relieved and thanked him for his kind understanding. As I drove towards the residence where my private students, two sons of a building contractor, were waiting for me, I mused that this happy resolution must be due to divine providence.

The second joyful reminiscence was the contractor's willingness to help me with a cash loan to settle my down payment with Yat Yuen Hong which sold me a semi-detached bungalow in Hongkong Park in Bukit Timah. He trusted me and told me to carry on teaching his two sons until the loan was paid up. Here again, I say this is divine providence!

I spent my weekends continuing my social life with a couple of close friends like Albert Goh, my school mate in St Andrew's School, the one and only school I had ever attended in Singapore. He became an assistant commissioner of Inland Revenue and got married much earlier than me. We used to drive to West Point where there was a night club. I met many young men and women of various professions there. It was a social environment where one could find many friendly people. It was there that I chanced upon a genial and charming young teacher. She introduced her friends to me at the table. After a witty conversation, I asked for her contact number and intimated that I might call at her home one day at a convenient time. She uttered: *"You are welcome."* From our confab, I gathered that she had two other sisters. Little did I realise from her welcoming response that she was going to introduce her eldest sister called Lucy at her home. Much to my surprise, I discovered that she was from a Peranakan family. Her parents welcomed me with open arms. Her sister Lucy had a pretty face but a rather thin body. They were a Catholic family. The father, who was teaching English in a nearby school, spoke excellent English and was quite an entertaining conversationalist. It was delightful to hear him talk. In fact, when I knew him well enough, I brought him the draft copy of my textbook for proof-reading. After a few days, I turned up and inquired whether there were any necessary corrections to be made. He could only spot one error, i.e. the 'a' in the phrase 'a common knowledge' ought to be deleted. He invited me to a Peranakan dinner with his family. I was introduced to his son whom I met for the first time, who was also a teacher. Lucy was unemployed and came across as a modest lady who was rather reticent. Her father remarked sympathetically: "*She is rather weak. She seldom goes out.*" I smiled at her, showing my understanding of her condition. Her mother was very friendly and spoke only Peranakan Malay to me. I spent a delightful evening with them. Before I left for home, I had a little chat with Lucy who was rather coy. As I was driving home, I began to muse on whether such a woman would make a good wife for me. "Only time can tell. God works in mysterious ways. Love is irrational," I reflected.

Most of the time I was busy with one thing or another. I could only visit Lucy on Saturdays. As for Sundays, she had to go to church with her family, followed by dinner outside or at home. As a non-Christian, I would spend the day with my friends on social activities in their homes where I would be invited for dinner. Sometimes, we would go to clubs to revel in tea dances, followed by dinner in restaurants or hawker centres. By sharing expenses, we were able to enjoy sumptuous meals. I lived this independent way of life as a bachelor, because I was alone and far away from my home in Kluang. By the grace of God, I never felt homesick. In hindsight, I believe that my decision-making was guided all along by divine providence.

As for Lucy, our rendezvous were infrequent, mainly because of my concern for her health. At one stage, I had on my own asked a doctor, whom I befriended in Newton where I relished the best char kway teow then in Singapore, to pay a visit to her home nearby. I said to him: *"Please don't mention my name. Just say that a friend of yours has asked you to examine her. I will pay the charges incurred."* The next afternoon, I invited the doctor to join me for char kway teow in the coffee shop next to his clinic. He revealed to me in confidence that she was suffering from a form of arthritis. He had prescribed painkillers for her. She insisted on paying for the treatment. When I next saw Lucy again in her home, she never mentioned it at all. I pretended not to know. She spoke to me about her love for music and songs. I asked what her favourite song was. She replied: *"Non Dimenticar"* meaning *"don't forget"* in English, an enchanting song sung in the movie titled "ANNA". I was impressed by her taste for music. She intended it for me, as a hint not to forget her. To her, probably I did not come across as a sentimental lover. I grew up from young to be manly and never to be a sissy.

As time passed by, I became more familiar with her. One evening, in a joyous mood, I took the liberty to take her to Stevens Guest House on the pretext of showing my room and the surroundings. When we entered the room, I was feeling amorous and could not help embracing and kissing her. I locked the door behind us without any protest from her. We lay down on the bed together and had our intimacy for the first time. Having experienced such ecstasy, we were naturally inclined to meet each other again. A couple of weeks later, when I did not contact her again owing to mundane occupations, she called me, expressing her desire to meet me again . I was excited by her desire and offered to fetch her that very evening. At the appointed time when I arrived at her gate, she was already standing there waiting for me. I drove her straightaway to my residence. After our moments of immense ecstasy on the bed, we sat up. I looked at my cupboard at the side, walked towards it and took out the diamond ring concealed therein. When I presented it to her, she was visibly touched and lost for words. I said: *"Keep this in remembrance of our love."* Strange as it might seem, neither she nor I talked about engagement. Our meeting was a secret tryst.

One late afternoon, I suddenly received a call from Lucy's second sister named Cecilia, who told me that Lucy would like to see me urgently at her home. I wondered why she herself did not phone me. I had a foreboding that she needed me to send her urgently to hospital. As soon as I arrived there, I asked Cecilia: *"What's the matter?"* She replied tersely: *"I don't know. She just asked me to call you urgently."* There was nobody else in the house. Then she pointed out the room where Lucy was lying. I thought she had taken ill suddenly and needed immediate hospitalisation. When she saw me, she smiled and beckoned me over to sit on her bedside. She whispered: *"I need you."* Knowing her intention, I instantly surveyed her big and bright room, which was not conducive to love-making at the time. I declined to do it. I suggested to her: *"Let's do it some other time in my place."* I could see from her countenance that she took my response very badly. On my part, I was being cautious and restrained myself from yielding to this temptation. After a while, I decided to depart. This moment caused her distress. I could imagine her brooding over it. After a fortnight, I received a call again from Cecilia who sounded ominous in her tone of voice this time. She requested me to turn up at 3.00pm. I did not know what was in store for me. As I walked up the steps, I was startled to see an open coffin at the veranda. When I finally reached it, I was shocked to see Lucy's corpse dressed in a white wedding gown. I was lost for words. I kept on staring at her face which appeared peaceful. Then Cecilia asked: *"Aren't you going to kiss her?"* I bent over and kissed her forehead, with tears welling up in my eyes. Surprisingly, nobody else was present at that hour except me and Cecilia. She revealed that Lucy would be buried in Bidadari cemetery the following afternoon. I told her I would be present at the cemetery to bid my last farewell to her.

It was by divine providence that I could carry on my life without bearing a heavy heart nor a grim sense of guilt. When I was transferred to teach General Science in Queensway Secondary School, life changed for the better by the grace of God. Margaret Tan, whom I depicted in Chapter 3, was a godsend to me. She was a lively personality who gave me great pleasure to engage with her.

Amazingly, the laboratory where I spent much of my time was located next to the class room where she taught Home Economics. This situation provided opportunities for us to meet more often. I still recall vividly one particular occasion when she sneaked behind me and placed her hands across my eyes while I was marking books. I was thrilled and turned around to behold her offering me some cakes. How heavenly!

She had been living with her elder sister Clara for many years since the death of their parents. She was educated by nuns in the Convent School at Middle Road. She was and still is a Catholic but I never perceived it as a hindrance to our relationship. Without our parents around us and being teachers who were financially independent, it was so much easier to make our personal decisions. As our relationship deepened, she decided on her own to move out of her sister's flat. Initially she rented a room from her colleague who lived quite near Queensway Secondary School. We agreed not to beat about the bush and head straight for our pure gold wedding rings. As a Catholic, she preferred to have a church wedding but the priest at the time could not agree to her request. So the only recourse we had was to have our marriage solemnised by the Registrar of Marriages, who set the date for 9th of February, 1963. By divine providence, Margaret's wish was fulfilled by the grace of God on 31st of July, 1971. We were 'united in holy matrimony' in the Franciscan Chapel Centre of Seisen International School, Roppongi, Tokyo. We were issued the Certificate of Marriage in Latin! I was posted there as a pioneer diplomat to help set up Singapore's 13th Embassy in August 1968. Our first residence was in Roppongi where Seisen International School was located.

Regarding our wedding in Singapore, we were greatly assisted by our friends Mr Stoner and Mr Low. My parents and siblings were happy to witness our solemnisation. Mr Stoner was my witness. We held our dinner celebration at a Chinese restaurant in New World. How amazing it is to note that we are now living on the same piece of land that was once called the New World! Moreover, my parents' wish for me to be educated in English and be married was finally fulfilled. If this is not divine providence, what is it then?

Celebration of Mr & Mrs Lim's Wedding 9 -2-1963 at New World. Now developed as a city within a city called City Square Mall & Residences where the Lims live now w.e.f. 13-4-2009.

CHAPTER 5

PROVIDENTIAL
CHANGE OF CAREER

After our marriage, we continued teaching in Queensway Secondary School. By divine providence, we were able to secure a rental flat from the Housing and Development Board (HDB). We moved out of Stevens Guest House in order to stay closer to our school. We led a blissful life. We were young and vigorous, and enjoyed our love life as before with the result that my wife was soon pregnant with our first child. We prayed for a son and God answered our prayers. I named him, Lim Tien, as a blessing from heaven (Tien). Chinese names usually have 3 characters just like mine, but I purposely had it reduced to 2 for a simple reason. This decision arose from my numerous examinations I took. On every examination sheet of paper, I had to write my full name so often until I swore to shorten my future children's names to 2 characters. Hence, after Tien, my wife prayed for a daughter and I named her, Lim Gek, whose second Chinese character means 'moon'. The following year came along a son whom I named, Lim Jit, whose second Chinese character means 'sun'. To me, it was utterly natural and easy to call them by their last names.

Moreover, it was very easy to write their names in Chinese characters unlike mine, e.g. 'Leong' meaning 'dragon' which is written traditionally in 16 strokes!

Incidentally, sometime in 1957, I was introduced to an old widow of Dutch descent, who was well-known among Eurasians in Singapore as a fortune-teller. First, she said a prayer and then asked me to pick a card. The one I picked showed a coffin. Then I was asked to pick a second card showing a wedding couple. This was relevant to my interest. When I inquired about the first card, she merely said that someone in my family would pass away. As to the second card, she predicted that the woman I would marry would not be someone born in Singapore. She looked at me for a while and asked: *"Do you believe me?"* Obviously, I appeared to be sceptical and said nothing in response except to give a forced smile. Then she remarked: *"Wait and see. Then you will know I am telling the truth today."* Quite surprisingly, the events that followed in the 1960s seemed to corroborate the two predictions that she made solemnly.

Regarding my father, I learnt from him in Kluang that a certain Chinese fortune-teller persisted in wanting to tell my father's fortune. Suspecting his mercenary motive, he refused him thrice. However, in his fourth attempt, my father relented out of pity for the poor fortune-teller. He foretold that my father would fall seriously ill at the age of 59. But if he could overcome it, he would survive. Before reaching 59, he suffered from Hodgkin's disease - a malignant disease affecting the lymphatic system. He died a miserable death in January 1967.

With regard to the second prediction, I actually married a woman born out of Singapore. This refers to my wife, Margaret Tan, whom I married on 9 February 1963. She was born in Muar, Johor. It was by divine providence that we met each other in Queensway Secondary School in Singapore.

After our marriage and blessed with three children, followed by the death of my father, there came into my life a new opportunity. My principal, Mr Ng Teng Law, sent a circular from the Ministry of Education inviting applications for foreign service posts. After consultation with my wife, I decided to put in my application. A colleague of mine, Mr Ghosh, also did the same. We were subsequently called up by the Public Service Commission for interview. By divine providence, I was successful while my colleague was not. After a week, I received an appointment letter requesting me to present myself at the Ministry of Foreign Affairs for training. It was newly set up just after our Independence in 1965. My appointment dated 13 May 1968 was actually a secondment from the Ministry of Education whereby my pensionable salary scale would be retained. As time was of the essence, my training was rather brief. I was then called up for an interview with the Director of Administration, Mr Herman Hochstadt. I was taken by surprise when he offered me a 6-year posting to Tokyo. As was generally known, the normal duration of posting was 3 years. Herman advised me to consult my wife who was still teaching and added that special leave would be granted to her if I decided to bring my whole family with me to Tokyo. My wife and I met for lunch at the Tang's Hotel at Orchard Road. She favoured the idea of moving to a foreign country. She was prepared to make sacrifices for the sake of my career. As we did not know what was in store for us in Tokyo, we decided to propose to Herman to let us try for 3 years in the first instance. By the grace of God, he agreed to our proposal. He came across as an understanding and helpful officer. I was pleasantly surprised when he told me that I would be the first administrative attache to be granted diplomatic status, thereby entitling me to a special but modest entertainment allowance apart from other allowances, such as clothing allowance for a full suit, school fees, medical expenses, accommodation, cost of living allowance but no dental reimbursement, much to my chagrin, as I discovered later in Tokyo.

Having completed my practical training in headquarters, I was instructed to study the set-up of our mission in Bangkok as well as in Hong Kong before proceeding straight to Tokyo to assume my duties. I arrived with my family on the morning of 8 August 1968 and immediately put up my family in Nikkatsu Hotel where our Ambassador's Personal Assistant Fong Fook Cheong and his wife were staying. Both of them whom I met for the first time were friendly and helpful. The following evening, Fong and I had to be present at our National Day Reception to usher our guests into the reception hall to meet our Ambassador and his wife. By the time I returned to my hotel with Fong, it was quite late in the night, and my children were fast asleep except my wife who was waiting for me. We stayed in the hotel for almost a month, because I had difficulty in finding suitable accommodation within my rent ceiling. In spite of this, I carried on with my duties with the assistance of Fong. In the months ahead, I was to work closely with Fong to resolve several administrative issues urgently.

CHAPTER 6
FIRST DIPLOMATIC POSTING IN TOKYO

Our Embassy was temporarily housed in the Imperial Hotel near the Imperial Palace. Fortunately, Nikkatsu Hotel was located near Hibiya Park where my wife would bring our children to play. This relieved me of my worry for their well-being while I concentrated on my occupation. I was operating without a receptionist or an accounts clerk nor even an office boy. In fact, I was expected to be a factotum. I was kept very busy every day.

Sometime in August 1968, Prime Minister Lee Kuan Yew came on an official visit to Tokyo. Part of the official programme included a visit to Hakone. In the morning, Ambassador Ang Kok Peng and First Secretary Sng Cheng Khoong accompanied PM Lee and his entourage to Hakone. Strange as it might seem, I was not told by anyone to expect a protest by Indonesian students in Tokyo. While they were away, the hotel manager came to my office to inform me that an Indonesian group of students in the lobby insisted on meeting the Ambassador. I exercised my discretion and told the manager to allow only the leader and one other protester to meet me in the lounge, because of space constraint. I received them with a smile to ease the tension. I asked them what they were unhappy about. They wanted Singapore to stop the execution of the two Indonesian KKO Marines. Initially they were persistent in wanting to meet the Ambassador. I informed them that we were in the Ambassador's suite and pointed out his bedroom. In order to convince them, I asked: *"Would you like me to open the room to let you see it?"* They responded tersely: *"No need."* I then spoke calmly: *"Since you are here to deliver the protest note, I suggest you hand it to me. I guarantee you that it will be forwarded to the Prime Minister."* The leader was somewhat pacified and agreed to hand it over. After a while, the duo stood up to make a move. I shook their hands and we parted amicably. The next day, I looked up the Japan Times and found a report about their successful delivery of the protest note to the Third Secretary, who assured them that it would be forwarded to the Prime Minister of Singapore. It was by divine providence that I managed to resolve a tense situation amicably. I had absolutely no experience in handling such a controversial matter.

Here I would like to record briefly that for the first time, I came into close contact with PM Lee Kuan Yew and Mrs Lee as well as their trusted aides, viz. Mr Wong Chooi Sen (Secretary to PM & Secretary to Cabinet), Mr Sankaran (Personal Assistant to PM) and Mr Tan Kah Wan (PM's Bodyguard). In the end, we became friends through our many official and personal dealings in a variety of matters. They found me a very useful conduit for their purposes in Tokyo. Is this not due to divine providence that I have outlived practically all of them to narrate the events in my life?

IMPERIAL HOTEL
www.imperialhotel.co.jp
21-10-19)
International Sales Offices: New York; Singapore

TOKYO

I was posted to set up the Singapore Embassy in Tokyo in August 1968. In July 1968, I was instructed by the Ministry of Foreign Affairs to study the set-up of the Singapore Embassy in Bangkok (see photos opposite) and our Consulate in Hong Kong. The interim Embassy in Tokyo operated from the suites in Imperial Hotel and subsequently relocated to the 32nd Floor of the first earthquake-proof building in Kasumigaseki Biru.

JAPAN TIMES AUG 1968

Singapore Embassy Gets Protest Note

Five representatives of the Indonesian Students Association in Japan handed a protest note to the Singapore Embassy Friday, concerning Thursday's hanging of two Indonesian Marines in Singapore.

Lim Chin Leong, third secretary of the embassy, received the note addressed to the visiting Singapore Prime Minister Lee Kuan Yew. The note said the Indonesian students here convey the Prime Minister their "strongest protest."

"The people of Indonesia and the New Order Government under President Soeharto had undertaken great efforts to cement closer relations and deeper understanding between our two nations" the protest note said. "In our view, closer relations and deeper understanding are possible only when both nations and governments are prepared to show a measure of humanism and humanitarianism."

Bambang Hidajat, secretary general of the association, said Indonesian students would be at Tokyo International Airport today when Lee leaves for Singapore to show their protest against the execution.

*Singapore Embassy in Imperial Hotel, Tokyo August 1968.
1st encounter with Indonesian student protesters.*

Another matter that bothered me was the urgent need for accommodation. The Ministry was hurrying me to seek a flat as soon as possible because I had exceeded the permitted period of stay in the hotel. Despite my difficulties, it was by the grace of God that in Roppongi, I chanced upon a vacant flat with two rooms and a dining-cum-kitchen room. The landlord refused my request to furnish it. My wife and I decided to furnish it with minimum furniture at our expense - an oblong dining table with only five chairs, a low Japanese table for the children's use in their room. All of us slept on the floor laid with tatami mats. My wife was willing to cook for some of my Japanese contacts at home, because it was too expensive to entertain them in a restaurant. I recall inviting the founder of Yomeishu (a Japanese tonic also exported to Singapore) to dinner with us at home. My wife, a Home Economics teacher, cooked a couple of Singapore dishes. I could see that he ate the food with great relish.

On another occasion when our Senior Minister of State Rahim Ishak was on his official visit, I personally invited him to my flat to introduce my wife to him. I had earlier on primed my wife to cook a special curry dish for him. He was pleased to see my wife who told him that she had specially cooked a curry dish for him. After he tasted it with relish, he said: *"It's delicious. Did you cook it with coconut milk?"* Smiling, she disclosed: *"Not at all. I used evaporated milk."* Rahim exclaimed: *"Marvellous! I'll tell my wife about it."* Three years later, when I was back in headquarters, I met Rahim again at an official function with a couple of our MPs. The first thing that he mentioned to them was my wife's curry, which he revealed was prepared without coconut milk. He asked them: *"Can you guess what she used?"* None of the MPs knew. Then he revealed: *"With evaporated milk, lah! It tasted delicious all the same."* They all laughed. It was a delightful moment for me.

When we were staying in Roppongi, another event occurred, much to my consternation. My wife revealed to me that she had prolapse of her womb. Her gynaecologist advised her to undergo surgery.

Fortunately, by the grace of God, my children were below school-going age and Mrs Fong kindly agreed to look after my children so that I could get on with my work. One afternoon, my wife rang me up to ask whether I had any objection to the lady surgeon's proposal to perform a reversible ligation that would prevent pregnancy. After a moment's hesitation, I consented and told her to go ahead with the operation. After a succession of three pregnancies resulting in her uterine prolapse, it was a sure sign to me that it was about time to stop 'production'. In hindsight, it proved to be a prudent decision as it relieved us of our worries and anxieties over monetary concerns and our quality of life, especially our health. Fortunately for me, I was still strong and had plenty of stamina. My wife's health improved after her surgery as she was able to do the household chores as well as coach the children. I would assist by bringing groceries for the family during my lunch hour. My children would be overjoyed seeing me bringing their goodies.

As my children were growing up, I felt that I should ask for a higher rent ceiling so that we would have more space, not only for the children's activities but also to meet the needs of my wife, such as hanging our increasing laundry. As a diplomat, I needed a decent space to entertain my guests. So I put up a comprehensive submission including photos which showed the flat to be rather cramped. Despite my Ambassador's strong support, my ministry seemed to be dilatory in its attitude towards my request. As there was no response in spite of my reminder, I decided to put up another submission detailing all my genuine and legitimate grievances with the ultimatum to send me back to my former ministry if my demands were not acceded to. As a result of this latest submission, I received a reply from a new director of administration by the name of Elizabeth Hon, daughter of Minister Hon Sui Sen. She returned my photos, assuring me that action had been taken and would inform me of the decision in due course. By the time approval was received, it was almost towards the end of my second year of duty. By the grace of God, we found a spacious apartment in Shinagawa according to our new rent ceiling. The building named Chateau Takanawa was located nearby the Shinagawa MRT and the Seisen International School where Tien and Gek studied in the primary school. We were happy staying here even though it was further from my office. I travelled to work by train while my wife sent the children to school by car.

Here I would like to narrate a little amusing anecdote which my wife related to me after the event. I received an invitation from the general manager of a large, newly opened hotel which was a stone's throw from my residence. The opening ceremony was in the afternoon. As I had a prior engagement, I asked my wife to attend it on my behalf. Conscious of the fact that she was a representative of Singapore, she dressed up in her attractive cheongsam. She looked well-endowed. At the reception, a certain Swiss gentleman approached her and took an interest in her. He introduced himself as a journalist who was stationed in Tokyo and tried to engage my wife's attention in conversation. As it was about time to leave for home to take care of our children, she excused herself and walked towards the exit. However, he kept pursuing her, asking for her phone number and address so that he could pay her a visit. In order to fend off his persistent attentions, my wife replied curtly:

"I am married with three children, you know. Please don't visit me." Then she hurried off in the direction of Chateau Takanawa.

Our Embassy had been searching for a piece of land to construct our own building instead of leasing properties. I recollect that the Venezuelan Embassy informed us that they had an additional piece of land which they were prepared to exchange for one in Singapore. It was in a good location and therefore we referred the matter of exchange to our ministry for approval. Our recommendation was forwarded to the Ministry of Finance for consideration but Finance Minister Dr Goh Keng Swee turned it down on the grounds that it was 'speculation'. Around this time, the first earthquake-proof building in Japan called 'Kasumigaseki Biru' was ready for occupation. We were fortunate to secure a lease for a big office space on the 32nd floor. We were assigned a flagpole on the ground floor to put up our Singapore flag. As our Embassy had the highest location among all other embassies, we earned the reputation of being the 'highest Embassy' in Tokyo. The Japanese press honoured us with this appellation. How amazing!

We started functioning on 15th of December 1969. As mentioned before, I was expected to be a factotum. My scope of duties expanded from administration and consular functions to tourism and trade. All along it was the Malaysian Embassy that issued visas on our behalf. I had to take over from them. The Japanese Travel News interviewed Ambassador Ang Kok Peng and me. As a result, I was saddled with the responsibility of issuing numerous visas. By the grace of God, I was able to recruit a lady receptionist, a translator, a visa clerk who doubled as an office messenger, a driver for the office car, a chauffeur for the Ambassador and a lady secretary to assist me in my functions including accounting. I must say that in my whole career, I had never come across such a dedicated and obedient lot of Japanese workers. In this regard, I was much influenced by the Japanese work ethic. Furthermore I recall an instance when a Japanese porter in a well-known hotel declined to accept my tip and remarked: *"No need, sir. I am glad to be of service to you."* Thereupon he bowed respectfully, to which I also reciprocated, and retreated out of the room. Another instance of culture shock to me was the deference of Japanese women to men, e.g. allowing men to enter the lift first before they did so, even though I was disinclined and waved them on. But they insisted, saying "dozo" meaning "please" by bowing and beckoning me to enter the lift. I felt a little embarrassed because I had been ingrained by British teachers to give way to a lady first. Incidentally, my wife found Japanese men, especially taxi drivers, rather brusque.

My visa section was generally busy and filled with visa applicants as well as official visitors. I had provided a long bench for elderly visitors. One morning as I was walking out to the toilet, I saw a humble, dignified-looking gentleman who smiled at me. When I returned, I smiled and asked him: *"What can I do for you?"* He replied politely: *"I am waiting for Ambassador Ang. I have an appointment with him."* As I had never met him before, I asked for his name. He responded humbly: *"Ho Rih Hwa from Bangkok."* His name immediately rang a bell, because I was supposed to call on him when I was at our Bangkok Mission. I informed PA Fong that Ambassador Ho was waiting quietly outside. Promptly Fong went out to receive him. His son Ho Kwon Ping is now the Chairman of Singapore Management University. Other notable visitors were Mr Dhanabalan, Mr Lee Khoon Choy and Mr Herman Hochstadt, whom I met again in Singapore. Mr Dhanabalan later became my Foreign Minister; Mr Lee Khoon Choy, Deputy Minister

Ambassador Ang & Consul Lim Interviewed at the Embassy by Japan Travel Bureau (Dec 1969).

under Minister S. Rajaratnam, after an eventful tour of duty as Ambassador to Indonesia; Mr Hochstadt, Permanent Secretary of Finance Ministry. I remember Hochstadt, who knew me well enough, wrote me a personal letter asking to receive him at the airport as he intended to stay overnight on his way back to Singapore. I met him again with his wife en route for San Francisco. My wife and I took the opportunity to have dinner with them at a Chinese restaurant owned by Y.Y.Sheng, my former colleague who taught English in Thomson Secondary School. Divine providence had brought us together after all those years. It is amazing! Similarly one of my best Chinese students named Chua Lam sought me out in Tokyo, much to my surprise. He joined Golden Harvest, a film production company in Hong Kong, as a script writer and made a name for himself. He is now a celebrated writer of culinary delights for a Chinese newspaper in Hong Kong.

My consular duties also included registration of Singapore ships, settling seamen's disputes as well as students' affairs. These duties sometimes necessitated travel out of Tokyo. I remember having to fly to Fukuoka in the southernmost island of Kyushu to settle a dispute between the crew and the captain of a Singapore-registered ship. While we were engrossed in the negotiations, the ship was slowly drifting out to sea. It was getting dark outside. By the grace of God, I managed to settle the dispute and immediately instructed the captain to bring me back to shore in order to catch the evening flight back to Tokyo.

On another occasion, I had to take a morning flight to Hiroshima to inspect a Singapore ship named Lion City prior to registration. By divine providence, I managed to take a quick tour of this historic city associated with its devastation by an atomic bomb dropped on 6 August 1945.

To inspect ship for registration at Hiroshima (May 1971).

The only bare structure with dome (behind me) as memorial of atomic devastation in Hiroshima on 6-8-1945.

I also recall vividly a weeping mother turning up at my residence on a Sunday morning, pleading with me to get her son, who was studying in Tokyo, released from the remand centre. The mother disclosed to me that her son had been arrested for theft in a supermarket. He was trying to get something urgently for his Japanese girlfriend even though he was short of money. In desperation, he resorted to stealing. Out of sympathy for the mother, I agreed to help. I could perceive the great relief on her countenance as she reposed her trust in me. The next morning I went to see the official in charge of the remand centre. By the grace of God, he was very understanding. He personally did not regard the boy's offence as a serious crime. He was willing to release the boy if I was prepared to sign the release papers. To me, I regarded it as my duty to help a Singapore citizen and therefore signed the forms without hesitation. The mother and the son were forever grateful for my good deed. As for me, it was a joy forever.

As for tourism promotion, I recall having the pleasure of receiving Miss Tourism Singapore at the Haneda Airport in 1969. She disembarked from the SIA plane attired in her costume with her sash displaying "1969 Miss Tourism Singapore". I accompanied her according to the programme of visits arranged by Singapore Tourism Board with assistance from the Embassy. I still have a photo of her taken together with me and my wife at an evening reception. I also remember taking her in a subway train to do a round trip in the city in the hope of raising Japanese awareness of the attractions of Singapore. In fact, I had been working very closely with the Japan Travel Bureau.

ASTA Convention in Tokyo with Miss Tourism Singapore 1969.
(L) My wife Margaret.

With regard to trade, the Embassy held an exhibition of Singapore products with Singapore manufacturers in attendance. The Japanese invitees showed great interest in our products and some of them placed orders on the spot. The Embassy also assisted in the participation of Singapore in Japan's first international expo in Hiroshima in 1970.

Here I would like to point out that Haneda Airport during my time was a transit point frequently used by our ministers and senior government officials travelling to the United States for meetings and conferences. The number of times I was requested to meet, receive and send them off at all times of the day was innumerable. Although it took up a lot of my time, I did derive pleasure from talking with them. They were appreciative of my assistance. Once I had to receive Dr Andrew Chew in my own car, as the office car was not available. When he arrived at the airport, it was quite late at night. I offered to drive him to his hotel which he had booked. Unfortunately our conversation distracted me and I drove in the wrong direction. I had to do a detour in order to reach his hotel. Both of us laughed it off. He remembered this funny mistake when we met again in Singapore. He later became Chairman of the Public Service Commission. We became friends in the end.

On another occasion, I had to receive Minister Ong Pang Boon who arrived late in the night from Singapore. There was evidently a miscommunication between Minister's office and the hotel's reception. Fortunately the Minister was able to produce documentary evidence of his PA's booking with the hotel. I had a word with the hotel manager on duty that night and by the grace of God, I managed to resolve the issue with him amicably. I informed him who I was, giving him my name card, and assured him that if he encountered any more problem with his 'higher-up', I would be readily available to assist him. As far as I know, a Japanese in authority could be a stickler for rules.

The next event I recollect would have landed me in the soup if not for divine providence. Minister Dr Goh Keng Swee and his delegation were returning to Singapore via Tokyo. I thought Ambassador Ang was going to receive him, but later on, he personally came to me and requested me to go to the airport to receive him on his behalf as he was busy. There was not much time for me to hasten to the airport, so I stopped work immediately. As I was on my way to the airport, the road was getting congested with cars. As I was anxious, I hurried the driver to overtake as many cars as possible. Every now and again I glanced at my watch and prayed to God to help me reach my destination safely on time. As the car approached the airport, the road was becoming less congested. I had only 15 minutes left before the plane touched down. My heart was beating fast. As soon as the car reached the VIP hall entrance, I dashed to the meeting area. Just as I reached it, I saw Dr Goh walking with his briefcase towards me. I smiled and greeted him: *"Welcome to Tokyo, sir."* He asked me: *"Where's Ambassador?"* obviously expecting him to turn up. I replied: *"He has an official engagement. So he asked me to receive you."* He did not appear glum as I walked him to the VIP room to wait for his flight back to Singapore. This was the first time I met him in person. Our paths crossed again when I was posted to London. High Commissioner Jek Yeun Thong asked me to receive him and his wife. This time he was on a private visit to see his son and his wife, particularly his grandson. He recognised me and appeared friendly.

I was due to relinquish my post on 11 August 1971. As far as my vacation leave was concerned, I was so preoccupied with my urgent tasks that I hardly consumed it with the result that I accumulated a lot of leave. As I was required to be back in Singapore by a certain date, I applied for a week's leave to spend my vacation with my family in Taiwan on the way back to Singapore. By divine providence, I was able to bring my children to a farm to show them cows, bulls and water buffaloes which they had never seen, and explained how these animals were used for the benefit of man. We also visited the beautiful national museum in Taipeh, where a lady guide related the history of Taiwan. Whereas my children were interested in artefacts, I was fascinated by the history of Taiwan. As a diplomat, I regarded the historical narrative as a 'crash course'. I learnt that Taiwan was originally inhabited by Malays and polynesians. The first settlers from China came in the 17th century. Named Formosa (beautiful) by the Portuguese, the island was the object of Spanish-Portuguese rivalry. A period of Chinese rule and renewed migration lasted until a Japanese takeover in 1895. In 1949, the Nationalist forces of Chiang Kai-shek were driven onto Taiwan by the Communist victory on the mainland. Under US protection, the authoritarian regime declared itself the Republic of China, and claimed to be the legitimate government of all China.

America's rapprochement with the mainland People's Republic of China lost Taiwan its UN seat in 1971 and US recognition in 1978. By the late 1980s Taiwan was moving cautiously towards democracy, although its international status remained problematic. With a guide, I did a sight-seeing round trip by train from Taipeh to Kaohsiung in the south via pauses in Taichung and Tainan. We ate Taiwanese food with great relish during our brief stops.

After my return to Singapore, I called on Mr Joe Desker, Deputy Secretary of the Ministry. He was glad to see me in good shape and asked about my family. Then he invited me to his office as he had something to tell me. After locking the door, he and I sat down to have a tete-a-tete. After taking his medication for heart ailment, he revealed that he was fully aware of my unhappiness with the existing service conditions. I disclosed to him that the allowances were so inadequate that I could hardly save any money. I added that there was no point in continuing my service if conditions were not going to improve. In response, he said that he would post me to another country soon, where I would be able to save at least 10% of my salary. But he could not disclose the country of posting yet. I took his word for it as I could sense his sincere effort to retain me as a valuable asset to the young ministry. I asked for his advice: *"Should I send my children to school in the meantime?"* Without hesitation, he advised me to let them play at home. *"It won't be long. You will receive an official notification from the administration soon,"* he replied. In less than three months, after waiting anxiously for it, I received official news of my next posting to India. In hindsight, it was a very good posting in spite of my initial misgivings. Deo gratias. (Thanks be to God.) My love for Latin was sparked from the time I studied it as a prerequisite for the BA (Hons.) in English of the University of London.

UNIVERSITY OF CAMBRIDGE

LOCAL EXAMINATIONS SYNDICATE

This is to certify that the candidate named below sat for a Joint Examination for the School Certificate and General Certificate of Education and qualified for the award of a

GENERAL CERTIFICATE OF EDUCATION

The candidate reached at least Grade 8 in the subject(s) named and attained the standard of the G.C.E. Ordinary Level pass where this is indicated.

LIM CHIN LEUNG   SO42   125

	Grade	G.C.E. Standard
LATIN	2	ORDINARY

SUBJECTS RECORDED   ONE   G.C.E. PASSES   ONE

EXAMINATION OF NOVEMBER/DECEMBER 1965

(See overleaf)   *A. L. Armitage*
                                              Vice-Chancellor

Compulsory Latin qualification for entry to
BA Hons(English) degree.

Experiences of Japanese style.

Experiences of Japanese style.

Vacation in Mt. Fuji with Japanese MFA Officer
(March 1971).

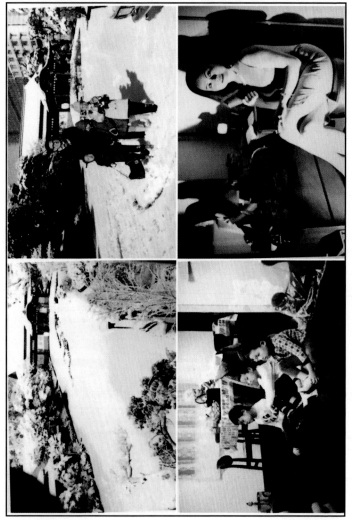

First experience of winter in Tokyo (1968).

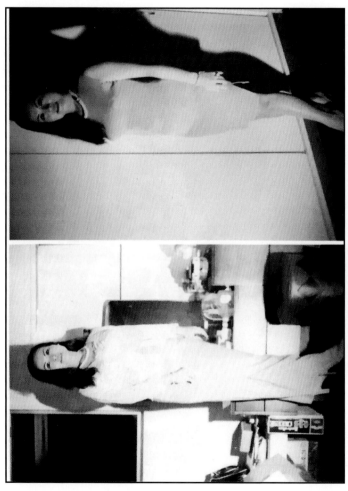

First experience of winter in Tokyo (1968).

Visit to Buddha in Kamakura to appreciate Zen Buddhism 9-8-1970.

CHAPTER 7
SECOND DIPLOMATIC POSTING IN NEW DELHI

I was required to travel by SIA to New Delhi via Bombay (Mumbai). We arrived at Bombay at night with several suitcases. We were advised to stay overnight at Bombay before proceeding by air to New Delhi. I was to report for duty on 25 November 1971. We had to take two taxis to the hotel. I took care of the luggage in one taxi while my wife took care of the children in the other. On the way to the hotel, my taxi broke down and we had to wait for another taxi in the dark. After some time, another taxi came by and my taxi driver spoke to the driver in Hindi for 'assistance'. Judging by their faces and behaviour, I felt rather suspicious, especially in the darkness of the night. I had my fears, so did my wife. We kept close to each other. The children were sleepy. We prayed to God for help in our hour of need. I watched my driver like a hawk loading my bags into the other car to ensure that none was left behind. I then paid him off without much argument. I told the driver who was with my wife and children to move ahead first while my new driver followed him. By divine providence, we got out of harm's way and reached our hotel safely.

When we arrived at New Delhi airport, my predecessor Michael Ting met us and took us to Lodhi Hotel which was our temporary accommodation. At the same time, the Indo-Pakistan war was still going on, much to my consternation. I worked overtime under curfew conditions, i.e. no light to shine out of my office through my curtained windows at night. I usually returned to my hotel by scooter taxi at 7.30pm. I did not feel comfortable in my new environment but nevertheless carried on because of my sense of duty. After nearly two weeks, I told my wife that I would send the family back to Singapore if the war continued. By divine providence, the war ended and the curfew was lifted. Michael Ting vacated his ground-floor apartment which I took over in a couple of days. He gave his big watchdog to me for guarding my apartment, which was quite large with a spacious backyard behind. What a contrast it was to my apartment in Chateau Takanawa in Tokyo. Moreover it was not expensive to employ a sweeper, a butler, and a female cook who doubled as my children's nanny. She was the only one allowed to stay with us, who eventually endeared herself to the children. I remember her name as Mrs Stella, who was highly recommended to my wife by Father Val De Silva of the Catholic Church in Greater Kailash near our residence.

One afternoon when I was all alone in the apartment, suddenly I heard a loud continuous banging on the door in the backyard behind. I also heard a loud voice of a man yelling in English to open the door. I held my watchdog by the neck collar and then opened the door. There appeared before me an Indian man with a menacing look, holding a crowbar in his right hand. Without showing any fear, I asked him firmly: "*What do you want?*" He replied abruptly: "*To check the sewer manhole.*" Thinking he was doing his duty, I allowed him in and stood some distance away from him with my watchdog next to me. He seemed to take his time and under my watchful eyes, he appeared to be surveying the area quietly. After about 15 minutes, he walked away without uttering a single word.

The whole event seemed weird to me. Following this weird incident, I attended a diplomatic function where I took the opportunity to make inquiries. I gathered from the Thai and Cambodian diplomats that robbery was rampant. They disclosed that they possessed pistols to protect themselves as they themselves as well as their homes had been accosted and robbed. Fortunately for us, by divine providence, we never encountered personally such incidents during my tour of duty in New Delhi.

One Saturday afternoon, I decided to take my wife to visit a big mosque in the city. As we entered the grounds of the mosque, a group of curious men, women and children began to trail along behind us, probably wondering where we came from, judging by the colour of our skin. They were staring at my wife, who felt very uneasy about it and urged me to go somewhere else. Then I took her to the city centre where there were many shops. As we strolled along, a number of children and women boldly touched us and some of them pulled our sleeves and begged for 'baksheesh' (tip). Since that day, we decided not to visit those areas again.

Every day, my wife would bring lunch in a tiffin carrier. One day, as she drove by a traffic junction, she saw a beggar sitting by the roadside, stretching out his hand for baksheesh. When she drove by the same junction on the way home, she saw the same beggar again and decided to give him baksheesh the next day if he was there again. Sure enough, he was sitting by the roadside. She approached him and handed him the baksheesh. She felt good about it. The following afternoon, she saw a couple of beggars at the same spot and thereupon she stopped to give the baksheesh. After the third day, more beggars turned up at the roadside, a few with sores on their feet. She took pity on them.

Feeling curious about the increasing number of beggars, I asked my local staff why there were so many beggars along the road. They remarked that many were not genuine beggars who saw it as a source of easy income. While I was not against my wife practising charity, I told her quite frankly to cease giving baksheesh, because we could not distinguish between genuine and bogus beggars.

When I was taking over the charge from Michael Ting, I noticed that he was quite brusque with the staff. After he left the mission, I decided to treat my staff kindly. My initial culture shock was that they still practised the caste system, e.g. the sweeper was not allowed to make a drink for the officers. Coming from Singapore and Tokyo, I found this repulsive. To begin with, I asked the sweeper to make drinks not only for me but also my guests as well as for all the other officers including the High Commissioner and their guests. Strange as it might seem, I also witnessed this colour discrimination whenever I accompanied High Commissioner Punch Coomaraswamy to receive VIPs arriving from Singapore. At the entrance, the Indian guard would stop him and requested to see his card, even though I identified him as my boss. As for me, it was quite plain sailing, without having to show my card, and he would just wave me on.

Talking about receiving VIPs at the airport, there was one incident which I remember vividly. Minister S. Rajaratnam was expected to transit New Delhi at a late hour at night on his return journey from Teheran. I was at the airport to meet him. I checked the passenger manifest with the airline executive. To my astonishment, his name was not there.

Nevertheless I waited for the designated plane to arrive. As soon as it landed, I sought permission to enter the plane to look for the Minister. As I walked along the aisle, my eyes looked at the seats on the left and right until I reached the end. There I found him reading a book quietly in the corner seat where there was space for me to stand and speak with him softly. After an exchange of pleasantries, I revealed that his name was not in the passenger manifest. To this he whispered: *"I am travelling under an assumed name."* At that time, there was news of terrorist hijacking on board.

There was an elderly Indian man who had been appointed by my predecessor as an 'office boy'. I found it rather inappropriate and therefore changed his official designation to 'Messenger'. He was earning a low salary and had a family of five. He also suffered from asthma and all of them lived in a ramshackle hut without proper cooking and sanitary facilities. It broke my heart when I saw this state of affairs. I decided to settle him and his family in an unused room at the rear of our premises. I found out one afternoon that he was also indebted, because a sympathetic staff member revealed to me that his regular visitor was none other than a money lender. I called him up one late afternoon to find out how much he owed the money lender. He said bashfully: *"2000 rupees."* I insisted that he settle his debt. For this purpose, I was prepared to help him personally with an interest-free loan which he managed to repay in small, affordable instalments. I also instructed him and the security guard not to permit the money lender to enter our premises.

There was a change of High Commissioners (HC), both of whom were political appointees. The new HC K.M. Byrne took over in the midterm of my service at the mission. By divine providence, his arrival gave me and my wife the opportunity to enter the Presidential Palace to witness the pomp and ceremony of HC Byrne's presentation of credentials to President Giri. First Secretary Peter Chan with his wife and I with my wife were formally introduced to the President. Photos were taken of this memorable occasion.

Seated L to R: Lim, Chatwal (Ch. Of Protocol), KM.Byrne (High Commissioner), Giri (President of India), Tivedi (Secretary, M.E.A.) Peter Chan, Kamtekar (Jt.Sec.). Group photograph taken immediately after Presentation of Credentials 20.7.73

As usual, my wife, who was conscious of her role as a worthy representative of Singapore, appeared resplendent in her silky cheongsam. No wonder President Giri's nephew took an interest in her when we met at a private dinner and dance in a well-known hotel in one of our many social gatherings in New Delhi. She was a good dancer and many diplomats including ambassadors enjoyed dancing with her. Even HC Coomaraswamy danced with her with a flourish, much to my surprise.

My wife Margaret being introduced to President Giri.

Ladies escorted down the palace steps. Margaret in resplendent cheongsam.

HC Byrne's first task to me was to replace the old Mercedes Benz. As he was fearful of the car parts being stolen, he instructed me to fly to Bombay and get our chauffeur to drive it to New Delhi. By the grace of God, we reached our mission safely at night. The second task was to purchase a duplex apartment in the hill resort of Nainital where there was a lake. This duplex was not only for the use of our mission staff during the hot summer but also open to other government officers from Singapore during the lull periods in the year. The third task was to get the mission's landlord to agree to change the system of monthly rental payment by cheque only instead of part cheque and part cash. Incidentally, there was a regulation that visa fees received locally were not permitted to be deposited into our external account. This compelled us to use up as much as possible the visa money collected, leaving the minimum sum in the petty cash box kept by me. With the aid of divine providence, I was able to keep my hands off the till. I would show him my petty cash book every month and let him count the cash in the box. My probity over time earned HC Byrne's trust in me. In fact, whenever he was away from mission, either on official visits to neighbouring countries or on vacation, he would personally authorise me to take charge of the mission instead of the First Secretary. In the fourth and last task, I raised the matter of purchasing a piece of land for the mission. I shared my Tokyo experience in this matter with him. I proposed that he meet the Secretary for External Affairs to find out whether there was a piece of land in Chanakyapuri which our government could purchase in order to erect our own building instead of leasing a property. Our bilateral relations were excellent. Soon after Mr Byrne's visit, he received the good news that a piece of land was available for sale. He was also informed of the price. He sought immediate approval and the necessary funds from our Ministry in order to seize the opportunity. The Ministry was prompt in remitting the funds into our external account with the Bank of India. Without delay, I prepared the cheque and signed it. Then I ran upstairs for HC to countersign. Both of us then walked down to the car which was waiting for him. As he entered the car, I wished him: "Good luck, sir." By divine providence, we finally secured that valuable piece of land. Before I relinquished my post on 20 December 1974, HC Byrne asked me to mark out the boundaries with four pegs according to the plan.

Here I would like to narrate a very important event in the life of my wife. One day, she had to return to Singapore to settle an urgent matter which required her presence. I told her to go alone and leave the children with me. By the grace of God, I managed to get a direct flight to Singapore on the same day and she reached her destination safely. However, her booking on her direct return flight to New Delhi had to be changed as the plane was grounded for an urgent repair. The only flight for the day which the airline could arrange for her return to New Delhi was via Bangkok. She reluctantly agreed to it. After she took off to Bangkok, the previous plane that she was supposed to travel on took off for New Delhi. As she did not inform me of the sudden change of flight, I merrily left for the airport to wait for her. She was supposed to arrive in the evening. After some time, I went to the airline counter to check the passenger manifest. To my astonishment, her name was not on it. Many people crowded at the counter, demanding to know why the plane did not arrive on time. Later on, the airline executive announced with sorrow that the plane had crashed into the sea and its location was being investigated. I could hear loud cries and thumping on the counter by irate family members. My heart sank when I heard the news. For the sake of my young children, I fervently and silently prayed to God to save my wife. I recalled the poet Alexander Pope's proverbial line of verse: *"Hope springs eternal in the human heart."* I then approached the airline executive to check another manifest for the name Lim Chin Leong Margaret. By the grace of God, he found it! Immediately I uttered *'Laus Deo semper'* (Praise the Lord God always). In response to my inquiry, he said that her plane was due to arrive in two hours' time. I waited patiently for her and finally she turned up safe and sound. It is amazing! This is divine providence.

My life in New Delhi was less taxing than my pioneering days in Tokyo. In fact, I had accumulated so much leave that HC Byrne was instructed to tell me to use up as much of my vacation leave as possible. So I took the opportunity to visit the Himalayas in the north where we learnt how to ride on horses. We also stayed in a boathouse called 'Biloo Palace' by a lake in Srinagar, Kashmir. We were served by a butler. One early morning, a boatman rowed me to the middle of the lake. As I lay down in the boat to enjoy the beauty of the surrounding landscape, I could imagine how the British Raj and his henchmen would have lived their lives. It was so much cooler than New Delhi. We also stayed in our government duplex apartment in the Nainital hill resort.

An Indian friend remarked: *"If you haven't been to the Taj Mahal and Khajuraho, you haven't seen the whole of India."* So we made trips southwards to see the famous Taj Mahal in Agra. It is a great monument to love. Built by Shah Jehan to the memory of his favourite wife, it is a celebrated example of Indo-lslamic architecture, the fusion of Muslim and Hindu styles.

On the way to Khajuraho, we stopped to explore the well-known fortress in Gwalior. As usual, we were impressed by the grandeur of the interior and the glorious lifestyle of the Maharajah. In 1858 the 22-year old Queen of Jhansi named Manikarnika dethroned the Maharaja of Gwalior for refusing to collaborate with her in her fight against the British. She refused to cede Jhansi to the British Empire. She was the first woman in the history of India to fight for Independence, but died in a fierce combat against British forces.

To visit Khajuraho, I invited an Indian friend named Babu who knew the route to my destination. While I was driving along the road, I saw an Indian girl trying to cross the road in a hesitant manner. As my car approached her, she suddenly dashed across my path and my right-wing mirror hit her when I swerved the car. I stopped the car immediately and got out to look for her. There she was lying on the road motionless. I exclaimed: *"God!"* clasping my hands

Visit to Taj Mahal in Agra (Nov 1971). Shah Jehan's great monument to love.

Visit to Taj Mahal in Agra (Nov 1971). Shah Jehan's great monument to love.

in prayer that she was not dead. It was a horrifying moment for me. I held her in my arms and a while later, a taxi came by and rushed her to the village hospital while I followed closely behind. When we arrived at the hospital, I was overjoyed when I heard that she was alive and suffered a minor injury. Meanwhile a crowd of curious onlookers surrounded my car. A policeman helped to disperse the crowd with his lathi. With the assistance of my friend Babu, we successfully negotiated with the village headman, in the presence of the girl's parents, an agreed sum of compensation in cash to be paid on the spot. Thereupon we left the hospital quickly in order to make it to Khajuraho before sundown. It was by divine providence that this untoward incident was resolved amicably.

In Khajuraho, we stayed overnight and the next morning we visited three temples with erotic sculptures of men and women in various sensual postures. I gathered that these temples were meant for tired warriors to relax apart from worshipping Hindu deities. After our lunch, we headed back for New Delhi. I could see in broad daylight cowherds lying by the roadside in the shade of the trees, enjoying their siesta. Their cows would also be in our way, thereby slowing down my car considerably. Soon night fell and I began to feel a little drowsy. In spite of my car light beams, I was veering the car towards a tree. I would have crashed into the tree if not for the alertness of Babu. His cry of "hey!" woke me up instantly, which made me swerve to avert the collision. My wife and children who were asleep were shocked by the sudden movement of my car. It was again by divine providence that we were saved. Thereafter I managed to get out of harm's way in our return journey to New Delhi.

One of my consular duties was to help Singapore citizens in difficulties whether financial or otherwise. Some of them were appreciative of my help and would report to my ministry my good deeds. A few of them, e.g. hitchhikers, who were stranded in India, would approach me for a loan to enable them to travel back by sea. My ministry rejected my proposal to use the petty cash to do so. So HC and I would personally loan them our own money out of compassion with the written undertaking that they would repay us after their return to Singapore. Hardly anyone of them did so, except for one particular individual whom I still remember honouring his promise. His name was Chiam See Tong, whose Volkswagen was impounded by the police at the Indian border. One morning I received a phone call from the Inspector of Police. He told me Chiam did not possess a carnet de passage. However, he was willing to release the car if I could assure him that he could produce it before he left India. I gave him my personal assurance just to help Chiam. On Sunday, he turned up at my residence and met my wife.

My instruction relayed through my wife was to meet me at my office early the next morning. When he appeared, he sought my assistance on two matters. The first one was to help him to contact urgently his family in Singapore to obtain the necessary carnet as soon as possible; and secondly, to lend him some money, as he had run short of funds. He told me that he was a teacher who had resigned to do law in London. After graduation, he and his girlfriend had travelled all the way from Europe to India until he committed the offence at the border. With that in mind, I agreed to help him. I loaned the sum of money he required to enable him to travel to Madras. He promised to repay the loan and expressed his gratitude for all the assistance I had rendered him. He was the first one to honour his promise. Years later, our paths crossed again when he was the only opposition member of the parliamentary delegation on an official visit to Kuala Lumpur.

CHAPTER 8

MY 3-YEAR STINT IN MFA HEADQUARTERS

On 21 December 1974, I returned to HQ to assume new duties in the political division. There I met Mr Rahim Ishak again. He was later appointed as Ambassador to Indonesia. I was appointed Country Officer for Indonesia, probably because of my academic qualifications in Malay, Jawi and Classical Arabic. Incidentally it was by divine providence that I had a natural interest in these subjects including Latin, which were all acquired in the 1960s long before I joined the foreign service. When I was studying Classical Arabic, I tried to buy a copy of the Koran, but the Arab Street bookseller refused to sell it to me when he discovered that I was not a Muslim! I was then a teacher teaching in Queensway Secondary School. So I asked a Muslim student in my class whether he could buy the Koran for me, because I was studying Classical Arabic for my Cambridge H.S.C. examination. He willingly got it for me! Who would have known that years later, all those languages would be applied in subsequent events in my life.

Mr Rahim never forgot how I treated him in Tokyo. Now that he met me again, he treated me like a good friend. So in my courier runs to Jakarta to deliver the diplomatic bag, he would ask his wife to prepare a special curry dish for me like what my wife did for him in Tokyo. It was a pleasure to discuss matters with him. Moreover, he had a great sense of humour. I recollect that I had to prepare a brief for him prior to his official visit to Papua New Guinea as he was also accredited to that country. After the brief was sent to him, I recall my director Barry Desker asking me to convey some last-minute instructions from the Minister. Rahim was quite appreciative of my effort to speak with him directly.

Another event that I recall vividly was the arrangement of an important meeting between the Australian Prime Minister Gough Whitlam and our PM Lee Kuan Yew. Our PM boldly expressed his displeasure at the racist policy of the Australian Government. This meeting was initiated by the Australian Ambassador on behalf his PM, who was trying to improve bilateral relations. By divine providence, I was instructed to attend the meeting, observe the atmosphere and make a mental note of the conversation. The two PMs spoke without facing each other directly, as they sat down in their chairs deliberately arranged to face me and the Ambassador. After the short meeting at night, I rushed home to prepare written notes from memory. As expected, my boss Tan Boon Seng asked for them first thing in the morning. After final vetting by the Minister, I submitted them to the PM's Office. By the grace of God, PM Lee accepted the notes without any amendment.

Another happy recollection was the occasion when I was instructed to go through a confidential technical document and summarise the content in good English, in not more than three pages. My command of English helped a lot and the final product was sent to the PM for his perusal. My boss, who was pleased, commended me for my good effort.

During my time, the Ministry of Foreign Affairs (MFA) was located in City Hall. I worked in the political division on the second floor. My desk faced the offices of Minister S.Rajaratnam and Deputy Minister Lee Khoon Choy. To enter the political division, one would need to pass through the main entrance door and then the inner door in a corridor. On rare occasions I would meet them at the inner door while exiting. One morning as I was exiting through the inner door, I unexpectedly saw Minister Rajaratnam walking towards me. With a smile, I greeted him: *"Good morning, Minister."* He reciprocated with a broad smile, recognising me, while I held the door open for him. To my surprise, he returned the courtesy by holding the door open for me to pass through. *"Thank you, sir,"* I said, impressed by his graciousness.

I also recall one occasion when Deputy Minister Lee Khoon Choy approached me at my desk and handed me a draft copy of his book titled "Indonesia - Between Myth and Reality". He politely requested me to go through it for English errors, omissions, typo errors etc. I found pleasure in it, as it was informative and edifying. It was based on true events in his tumultuous years as Ambassador to Indonesia. We had met each other at the Tokyo Mission in 1969. By divine providence, this place gave me several opportunities to come in contact with notables. It was here that I met Mr S.R.Nathan every now and then. He would come to brief Minister or get personal instructions from him. In this way, he got to know me very well.

When he became High Commissioner to Malaysia, he treated me like an old friend. We worked very closely together. He found me a very valuable asset to him, as I was his 'eyes and ears'. He was instrumental in getting me transferred from London to Kuala Lumpur when he became the Permanent Secretary of MFA. In fact, he chided the administration for wasting my talents in London.

Another notable I met was Mr David Marshall whom I admired as a brilliant criminal lawyer. Knowing him as an opposition leader, I was surprised to meet him in the corridor. He told me in a brief exchange that the Minister wanted to have a chat with him. He was curious about the purpose of Minister's invitation. He thought that I would know something about it since I was working on the same floor. I gave him a negative response. To this, he remarked cynically: *"Maybe, he is trying to recruit me into the PAP!"* I chuckled at this, seeming incredulous. Anyway, in hindsight he was offered a political appointment as Ambassador to Paris. When I was posted to London, I met him again and was given the opportunity to drive him all the way to his home in Brighton, a seaside town in the south. This long trip gave us the chance to know each other very well. In his private legal practice, he came across as someone who was very good at criminal law, but rather poor in his administration of the firm's finances. A lady colleague of mine had to help him keep accounts of his personal expenses in Paris. He was fond of patronising a Parisian nightclub for entertainment. Our paths crossed again when I returned to HQ for the last time. He and his wife were invited by MFA Club to give a talk to the officers.

There were other political appointees whom I met in City Hall, such as ambassadors. I recall particularly my chance meeting with Mr P.S. Raman at the basement of City Hall, my usual exit and also the drop-off point of Minister's car. We had not met each other since I left St Andrew's School in 1955, the one and only school I had ever attended in Singapore. Therefore, it was by divine providence that I met my teacher again. He taught me General Paper for the Cambridge H.S.C. exams. What I particularly remember about him was his kindness in trying to get me a scholarship after the death of my aunt, who was my benefactor. While I satisfied the criteria of eligibility in other respects, I was disqualified under nationality, because I was a Johor national. I did not know that he had joined the MFA in 1968 when I was posted to Tokyo. He mentioned that his first posting was to Indonesia where he had a tumultuous time because of the hanging of two Indonesian marines, who were regarded as war heroes as a result of their successful attempt to explode a bomb in MacDonald House in Orchard Road. (q.v. my detailed description in Chapter 6 of the Indonesian students' protest in our Embassy in Tokyo during PM Lee Kuan Yew's official visit.) He added that he was then Ambassador to Moscow and was back on leave for consultations with the Ministry. That was our last chance meeting because he died of a heart attack in Moscow. By divine providence, during my second and final return to HQ in 1991, I worked closely with his son, Mr Bilahari Kausikan, Director of Southeast Asia Division. By then, MFA had moved to Raffles City Tower with its magnificent view of Marina Bay and harbour.

When I returned from New Delhi in December 1974, I called on Mr Joe Desker, Deputy Secretary of the Ministry and presented him a book about Indian diplomacy and protocol, which I believed would be useful for him. He appreciated my gesture. Then he asked me how I felt about my posting to New Delhi. I told him frankly that my family and I experienced initial difficulties due to the ongoing Indo- Pakistan war. I had thought of sending my family back to Singapore if the war continued. However, by the grace of God, the war ended in about two weeks and things returned to normal after the curfew was lifted. Our Minister also inquired about the welfare of our students, particularly his nephew Vijay who was doing his medical studies. We assured him that all of them were safe. I remember particularly three of them who often kept in close touch with me and First Secretary Low Choon Ming, viz. Vijay, John, George Abraham. Only George who is now a businessman in Singapore still keeps in touch with me. I also thanked Mr Desker for sending me to New Delhi, because I was able to save at least 10% of my salary as he had promised me. My life was much better than that in Tokyo. Therefore, in January 1973 when MFA offered to 'absorb me into the foreign service', I consented after consultation with my wife as both of us were already pensionable officers.

I was also happy to meet Choon Ming again, who was then the Director of Administration. We first met in New Delhi in November 1971. As colleagues, my wife and I offered to look after his three young children so that they could attend their official functions with peace of mind. We became friends in the end.

Sometime in August 1977, I was due for another overseas posting. Choon Ming approached me in order to sound out my reaction towards a posting to Kuala Lumpur (KL). I told him frankly that I would be grateful if I could get a posting to London, because KL was near and I could easily afford to bring my family there without much expense, whereas my dream to go to London was truly difficult to fulfil. I suggested that perhaps MFA could post me to KL thereafter. He evidently put in a good word for me, because later on, the Permanent Secretary Mr Chia himself phoned me to say: *"It is my decision to post you to London."* This is divine providence.

Mr Lim remembers his good old friends, L to R: Mr Low Choon Ming, Mr Kok Ah Wang, Mr Tan Ban Cheng from Penang (April 2016) Marriott Tang Hotel, Singapore.

During my stint in HQ, I was one of the officers selected by Mr Joe Desker to attend courses on international finance, history, politics and economics at the University of Singapore. Equipped with that knowledge, I was posted to London in September 1977.

CHAPTER 9
THIRD DIPLOMATIC POSTING IN LONDON

It was by divine providence that I got a posting to London. After the official handover of duties between me and my predecessor, I moved into the latter's 2-storey semi-detached house which was about a hundred years old, as most of the houses were in those days. It was situated in an area called Golder's Green where most of the Jews lived. There were also many Indians who owned houses there. We liked the area with its many beautiful gardens and a large playground. However, my wife experienced a real culture shock when she first visited a grocery store. She was rudely told off by the Jewish grocer not to pick and choose the fruits and vegetables. Our garbage collectors expected to be tipped if we exceeded the quota of two bagfuls of rubbish. Furthermore, during Yuletide they would come to collect gifts of money and a bottle of whisky. When they went on strike, my wife had to discharge our garbage at a collection point some two miles away from our home. Taxi drivers expected to be tipped in addition to the payment of the meter fare regardless of whether you were happy or not with their service.

Family photo taken at front of residence 59 Cheviot Gardens, Golders Green, North London in winter.

Our High Commission building at 2, Wilton Crescent, was leased from Lord Mountbatten, notable for being commander in chief in Southeast Asia in 1943 and the first Governor-General of India until 1948.

Apart from my usual consular and administrative functions, I was given the additional responsibility of paying the pensions of colonial officials who had served in Singapore. I was given the mandate by the Accountant-General of Singapore to hand over the responsibility to the British Government during my tenure.

Meanwhile, I carried on my role as a pension paymaster. Some of the pensioners wrote to me to get the exchange rate revised from S$1.00 = 1 shilling 4 pence to a better rate. Our Accountant-General replied that it could not be done because it was already laid down by the British Government by a Constitutional Order-in-Council. This event reminds me of their hubris that the 'Sun' (i.e. Great Britain) would never set in the East. I remember my history master Mr Krishnan telling me of his intention to write a book about this British perception of their Empire. In this connection, I recall vividly receiving an unexpected call from Sir William Goode, the last Governor of Singapore, seeking an appointment with me. Thinking he was coming to collect his pension, I replied courteously: *"Sir William, there is really no need to come all the way from Reading to collect your pension."* He responded humbly: *"Mr Lim, since I know you only by name so far, I thought I might as well call on you, as I have some business to attend to in the city."* To me, my unexpected meeting with him was by divine providence.

Apart from him, I also met Prof. Jayakumar who was in London to do some confidential research. I remember providing him with a table and chair in a room next to mine. That was the first time I got acquainted with him. Our paths crossed again in the Singapore Golf Club where our MFA officers had a golf competition with their Malaysian counterparts. He recognised me and we had a friendly chat in a relaxed atmosphere. Subsequently he became my Foreign Minister. By then he knew me well enough. I have currently in my possession a scroll of commendation signed by him and a photo of me receiving a National Day award 'Pingat Bakti Setia' (PBS) from him. PBS is only awarded to those who have served at least 25 years of 'irreproachable character'. My last encounter with him was at our Embassy in Cairo where he asked me: *"I heard that you are retiring soon."* To that I replied exultantly: *"Yes, sir."* He smiled at me. Cairo was my last posting where I retired officially on 25 June 1996, i.e. on my birthday! Incidentally I also received a valedictory letter duly embossed from President Ong Teng Cheong expressing gratitude for my long and loyal service and wishing me a happy retirement. All this is divine providence.

Mr Lim Chin Leong Receives Award Of
Pingat Bakti Setia (PBS) / Long Service Award
From Minister Of Foreign Affairs Prof. S. Jayakumar
On National Day 1993

See red embossed seal in frame (left). Valedictory letter from President Ong Teng Cheong thanking Mr Lim Chin Leong for his loyal and dedicated service to Singapore and wishing him a happy retirement (June 1996).

Divine providence also gave me a chance to know a very interesting personage by the name of Devan Nair. As a teacher, I had heard of his political activism. I admired his cardinal virtue of fortitude. I recall the instance when he resigned as Political Secretary over policy issues with the Education Minister and returned to St Andrew's School to teach. He and my namesake Lim Chin Siong, among others, were detained by the British Government for being 'troublemakers'. After the PAP won 43 out of 51 seats at the Legislative Assembly general election on 30 May 1959, Governor William Goode asked Mr Lee Kuan Yew to form the first fully elected, post-colonial government. With regard to this event, I correctly predicted the number of PAP seats and won singularly the stake against my colleagues in Queensway Secondary School. PM LKY got Devan Nair, Lim Chin Siong and six others released. My personal relationship with Devan was forged in London during his annual visits to see his sister. I would offer to drive him in my car as well as present him with a bottle of whisky. After my marriage, I gave up smoking 'Du Maurier' cigarettes and drinking. When I was in Kuala Lumpur (KL) in the 1980s, I was astonished when he as President, accompanied by HC Maurice Baker, suddenly turned up one afternoon at my office. Maurice stood outside my door while he had a little chat with me. Divine providence had brought us together again.

There were numerous Singapore students spread out in different parts of Britain, viz. England, Wales, Scotland, Republic of Ireland and Northern Ireland. Regarding Northern Ireland, I remember reading about our landlord Lord Mountbatten who was killed by an Irish Republican Army bomb aboard his yacht in county Sligo.

During my tenure, as a matter of Government policy, the Education Ministry decided to recruit native teachers of English. In this regard, I was tasked together with another officer Koh Yong Guan from the Education Ministry. Mr Koh later became the Commissioner for Inland Revenue. I recollect that we together with Director of Education Chan Kai Yau had to make an exceptional trip to Dublin (capital of Republic of Ireland) to interview a few Irish teachers of English. As a trainee teacher, I recall several of my lecturers speaking English with different accents, i.e. Oxbridge, Welsh, Scottish, Irish.

I was fortunate that a special unit catering to the various needs of our students had been formed in another building at 5 Chesham Street nearby. It was managed by another MFA officer Mohinder Singh whose dealing with me was mainly financial. There was also a special officer to take care of PM's second son Lee Hsien Yang who was studying in Cambridge University during my tenure. His parents would make annual private visits to see him. That was when I would meet him with his parents at the airport. I remember distinctly one occasion when I had to bring his parents to Hyde Park Hotel which Minister S. Rajaratnam had recommended. As anticipated, I was able to answer promptly when PM LKY asked me in the lift about the hotel and who recommended it. I occasionally visited this park to listen to various types of speakers standing up on wooden boxes to express their views about God and Christianity, politics, economics, philosophy etc. I found it fascinating and edifying.

My scope of work began to expand to cover the fields of politics and information about Singapore for distribution to public inquiries. I was familiar with this kind of work. I managed to befriend the Secretary to the Parliamentary Speaker George Thomas. As a result, I was able to attend a couple of parliamentary sessions for first-hand reporting. I also gained further experience from attending Asean meetings. The most important meeting was the Conference on Rhodesia held at Lancaster House in London under the auspices of UK Government. Rhodesia was then divided into North Rhodesia named Zambia and South Rhodesia called Zimbabwe. Divine providence gave me the opportunity to meet with two great African leaders, viz. Robert Mugabe, Joshua Nkomo. They were waging a political struggle against PM Ian Smith, founder of white Rhodesian Front. The white-dominated regime detained both of them for a decade. After their release, they joined forces as joint leaders of the Patriotic Front in 1976. The Lancaster House Conference eventually led to Rhodesia's independence as the new state of Zimbabwe. Mugabe became the President and Nkomo the Vice-President. I remember President S.R.Nathan was invited by President Mugabe to make a state visit to Zimbabwe long after my retirement.

Another event in my life, which I attribute to divine providence, was the opportunity to meet Queen Elizabeth ll and her consort Prince Philip in Buckingham Palace. Most of the people could only view Buckingham Palace from the outside. This opportunity was afforded when HC Jek Yeun Thong together with his diplomatic staff had to attend a ceremony for the presentation of his credentials to the Queen. At the appointed hour, the state landaus would arrive at the High Commission to fetch us including our wives to Buckingham Palace. We were duly attired in our white tie and tailcoat while our wives were in their national dress or cheongsam. As I walked up the steps towards the ceremonial chamber, I quietly observed the many Ming vases displayed in the niches along the wall. My curious mind wondered whether they were presented by the Chinese emperors or

*Dressed up to be taken by state landau to Buckingham Palace
to see Queen Elizabeth during Presentation of Credentials by
High Commissioner Jek Yeun Thong.*

plundered from the Imperial Palace, e.g. the renowned Summer Palace in Beijing. Only the men were required to be present at the ceremony. The Lord Chamberlain advised us how to approach the Queen by walking three steps forward and retreat three steps backward before turning to depart. When the grand doors opened, we saw the Queen with Prince Philip next to her. HC Jek advanced to present his credentials which Her Majesty accepted. Then HC introduced us to the Queen and Prince Philip. I overheard Prince Philip making a humourous remark: "*So these are your workers.*" The Queen smiled as HC merely nodded his head with a forced smile. Our wives including Mrs Jek, who were waiting in a nearby chamber, were not presented to the Queen in contrast to the Indian protocol whereby HC Byrne introduced the wives to President Giri.

I recall receiving an official invitation from the Grand Chamberlain "requesting the presence of Mr C.L.Lim and Mrs Lim" to attend a dinner and dance at Buckingham Palace. It was a formal occasion where we met several diplomats from other missions in London. Incidentally I decided to contract my name to avoid being addressed as 'Mr Chin' or 'Mr Leong'. We also received official invitations from the Grand Chamberlain to attend the Queen's annual Garden Party where we interacted with diplomats and their wives as well as the Queen's guests. Practically all of them whom we conversed with knew about Singapore and its leader Mr Lee Kuan Yew. They would ask us whether we had gone on sightseeing tours in the country. We shared our impressions of the cities and seaside towns we had visited. I remember distinctly a tourist spot called Tucktonia outside London, which was specially created to showcase the best of Britain in miniature, i.e. all the famous landmarks in Britain. This place of interest reminds me of a similar place called Madurodam in the Netherlands.

The British are proud of their traditions, e.g. they maintain maps of historical England, Wales and Scotland as well as celebrate their old traditional festivals. They also keep up with scientific developments in the world. In the realm of academic studies, especially the humanities require a basic knowledge of Latin or Greek and a lot of memory work. The University of London, for instance, conducts external exams for private candidates who are unable to be full-time internal students, just as in my case. But the academic rigours and the standard of final assessment remain the same. For example, for my final BA (Hons) degree exams in English, I had to sit for ten papers of which a failure in one would result in a retake of all the papers. By the way, the English Language papers consisted of Old English including translation, Middle English and New English besides other papers such as literary criticism and analysis, which was a real 'killer' for most of the candidates comprising teachers and school principals. Because of my diplomatic functions, I could only find time to sit for my exams in Singapore. By the grace of God, I was the only candidate from Singapore who was conferred the degree.

A diplomat is expected to explore the country of his posting. In this regard, it was by divine providence that I was able to spend two weeks of my annual vacation with my family during the summer school holidays. Moreover, the sun would be still up in the sky until 8.00pm. I recall making a round trip through England, Wales, Scotland and straight back to London in the second year of my posting. I drove westbound from London. I was told that there were many hotels along the way. If they were fully booked, I could find lodgings with bed and breakfast. Therefore I did not bother to book any accommodation in advance. By the grace of God, we could find either type of accommodation, even

With my 3 children (R - L) Tien, Gek, Jit after receiving my BA (Hons) degree scroll at the University of London.

as late as 8.00pm. Rarely did we encounter any snag, e.g. racist attitude or unreasonable behaviour of the property owners. Most of them enjoyed talking with us after realising that we were not Koreans, Japanese or Chinese from China. The rustics particularly were ignorant of our nationality. We would enlighten them about Singapore as a multiracial, multicultural and multi-religious society. Surprisingly, only in U.S.A. did we hear a couple of American youths in Disneyland asking whether Singapore was in China. When my wife remarked that they did not know their geography, they scoffed: *"We don't need to know Singapore."*

As a student and trainee teacher, I was imbued with the illustrious British culture and glorious victories of the British Empire. The Empire was at its largest at the end of World War I, with over 25% of the world's population and area. Here I would like to relate one incident that has remained in my memory until now. This incident took place in Kluang, Johor. I was about 17 years old when I encountered an officer of the British Military Administration in Malaya. It happened at the Kluang Post Office where my classmate Ali was working. I did not realise that the British officer was standing a little distance away from me. After greeting Ali and inquiring about his health, he pointed to the officer waiting to be served. On realising this, I apologised thus: *"I am so sorry, I do apologise."* This was not acceptable to him and he threatened me: *"People like you ought to be shot!"* Another incident which I wish to add was when, as a school boy, I was given a couple of slaps on my face when I entered a swimming pool nearby my school, which was meant for British officers. Be that as it may, they have not changed my esteem for the strict discipline of the British Military Administration (BMA). In fact, as a diplomat I was invited to attend a ceremonial passing-out parade at Sandhurst

Royal Military Academy and came away impressed by its highly disciplined march-past. It was indeed a memorable visit for someone like me.

With prior knowledge and a detailed travel map, I was able to locate quite easily the various places worthy of a visit. Besides those forementioned, I also drove to Greenwich where I explained to my family the Greenwich Mean Time (GMT), i.e. the local time at the line of 0 degree longitude, which passes through Greenwich in England, used to calculate times in most other parts of the world. The Greenwich meridian line was clearly marked on the ground. I also took them to William Shakespeare's home and enjoyed the cool, calm, beautiful landscape of the River Avon.

My favourite Shakespearean sonnet is this:-
(1st quatrain + ending couplet)

"Shall I compare thee to a summer's day?
Thou art more lovely and more temperate:
Rough winds do shake the darling buds of May,
And summer's lease hath all too short a date:
* * *
So long as men can breathe and eyes can see,
So long lives this and this gives life to thee."

I then moved on to North Cornwall heading along the western coast for Tintagel Castle and Museum to learn about the legendary King Arthur and his 150 knights who sat at his famous Round Table. I was scolded for taking a photo of it. The guard allowed us in with my camera, so I thought that photography was permitted. We did not stay overnight at Tintagel but proceeded straight to Wales where we sojourned at a town called Ffestiniog, as it was getting dark. The next morning, we took a conducted tour to Blaenau Ffestiniog to see the largest slate mine in the world called Gloddfa Ganol Slate Mine. There were 30 levels in the mine which extended from around sea level to 1600 feet with over 42 miles of tunnels and hundreds of chambers inside the mountain, largely hewn by hand, by generations of miners working by candlelight. Samuel Holland was one of the pioneers who developed the narrow gauge railway and Porthmadog Harbour. I have a photo of our visit taken in a tunnel in August 1980. I was 44 years old then, still vigorous and alert. After our lunch in the slate mine, I drove on without a break to Edinburgh, capital of Scotland. After a brief tour of Edinburgh, a cultural centre known for its annual festival of music and the arts, I visited the old house of John Knox, Protestant reformer, founder of the Church of Scotland. He spent several years in exile for his beliefs, including a period in Geneva where he met John Calvin, French-born Swiss Protestant church reformer and theologian. Knox returned to Scotland in 1559 to promote Presbyterianism. We sojourned at a bed-and-breakfast lodging where we enjoyed the company of our host. He was impressed by the way we spoke English, which he described as 'Queen's English'. We told him that we would appreciate eating salmon, but he regretted that he was unable to provide it, so he suggested trout. We agreed readily as we were hungry. He served us a very delicious dish of trout which we ate with great relish. Early the next morning after our substantial breakfast, I drove southbound through the highway non-stop to London, reaching it before sundown - a distance of about 1000 km - without any mishap. Divine providence guided me out of harm's way. Laus Deo!

By divine providence, my family and I were able to make a similar round trip by our car through three countries, viz. France, Belgium and the Netherlands (or Holland). My children were then secondary students in St. Mary (Church of

England) School. Incidentally the body of Stamford Raffles was buried behind the school. Their second language was French which came in useful during our stay in Paris. The French were very proud of their language and some of them refused to speak English with us. Our purpose was not only to enjoy sightseeing but also to understand their history and culture.

I drove Southeast from London to Dover where we boarded the hovercraft to cross the Strait of Dover to Calais. It was an exciting first experience for us. I still have a video recording of our trips to the three countries. Owing to time constraints, we could not visit as many places as we would have liked to, such as museums. So we visited only the notable features of the capital cities. In Paris, for instance, we climbed up the steps of the famous Eiffel Tower up to a certain height to view the surroundings at the lower level and then took the lift to the top of the Tower for an overall view of the environs. Following that visit, I drove to the Champs-Élysées leading to the Arc de Triomphe where we boarded the lift to the top to view the whole city. By the grace of God, we enjoyed a clear and magnificent view of the city. Before sundown, we looked for a boarding-house called 'pension' in French. It was quite commodious and had a rather small shower bath. We had some difficulty in communicating with the lady owner who spoke only French. Fortunately my younger son Jit was able to clarify for us in English as to the rental terms and conditions.

The next morning, I drove the family to the Place de la Concorde, the city's largest public square with a lengthy history. The period between 1789 and 1795 saw the end of the monarchy and its claim to absolute rule. It was the site of the guillotine that was used to execute King Louis XVI and Queen Marie Antoinette. She was the daughter of Empress

Maria Theresa of Austria. Queen Marie helped provoke the French Revolution of 1789. After this visit, I drove on non-stop to Brussels, capital of Belgium. I called on my colleague Ms Lee Yoke Kwang of the Singapore Embassy, who arranged for our accommodation. She also invited me and my family to dinner at a French-speaking restaurant. She also made an appointment for us to visit a diamond-cutting industry in Antwerp, one of the world's busiest ports. Brussels is an industrial city. It is the headquarters of the European Community and since 1967 of the international secretariat of NATO. After seeing the 'atomium structure' and the park, we proceeded towards the Netherlands.

As there was time, I headed straight for Keukenhof renowned for its tulips. It is situated southwest of Amsterdam. The name Keukenhof (Dutch for 'kitchen garden') was originally derived from the name of the castle which belonged to Countess Jacqueline. The Keukenhof exhibition park was established in 1949 by the then Mayor of Lisse. Other countries in Europe were invited to show off their hybrids. Today Holland is the world's largest exporter of flowers. It was such a marvellous delight to stroll among the numerous variegated flowers! We felt refreshed not only by the cafe's drinks but also by the brilliant and vibrant colours of the surrounding flowers. Much as we wished to linger in the huge flower garden, we had to hasten towards our destination Amsterdam before nightfall. On arrival, we managed to find an Indonesian hotel where we enjoyed its Indonesian dishes with great relish. As we were quite fatigued, we went to bed early. Our next-day programme was to visit the Zuider Zee, a former sea inlet in Holland, cut off from the North Sea by the closing of a dyke in 1932, much of which had been reclaimed as land. The remaining lake is the IJsselmeer which had been turned into fresh water since

1944 over an area of 1,217 sq. km. Singapore has utilised some of its technical expertise.

As I was nearing the end of my vacation leave, I took a shorter route back to Calais via Rotterdam in Holland, Oostende in Belgium, Dunkerque (or Dunkirk in English) in France, and finally Calais. All are located along the northern coast of Europe. I had intended to stop by Dunkirk because of its historic significance during the 2nd World War. Many historians say it was the battle at Dunkirk that cost Germany the 2nd World War. In his famed speech in 1940: *"We Shall Fight on the Beaches"*, Winston Churchill, *Britain's Prime Minister called it a "miracle of deliverance"*. Initially it was thought the Nazi Germans would reach the beach within 2 days, allowing time for only 45,000 British and French Allied troops to be evacuated to safety. Instead 338,226 troops were remarkably evacuated from the beach and harbour at Dunkirk. Anyway, by divine providence, we returned to London without any mishap. Laus Deo!

London seemed to me to be the right place for me to pursue my interest in law. My interest in law had been piqued by my association with David Marshall and Stoner Kadirgamar, a good friend who officially witnessed our marriage as well as a veteran lawyer from Sri Lanka (Ceylon). Moreover, my diplomatic work involved compliance with government rules and regulations as well as international laws. By virtue of my London University degree, the Council of Legal Education admitted me as a student of the Honourable Society of Gray's Inn and issued me a yellow card to attend all the compulsory dinners of the Society. There are four Inns of Court in London, viz. Gray's Inn, Lincoln's Inn, Inner Temple, Middle Temple. They train law students and have power to call them to the English bar. There is a common examination board. Each Inn is under the administration of a body of Benchers (i.e. judges and senior barristers). I noticed that Gray's Inn comprised graduates from Universities of Cambridge, Oxford, and London. I found the tradition fascinating, i.e. students dressed in black gowns with half or full sleeves, dining and toasting in fours at tables and benches made of oak, using rather large forks, spoons and plates. In the presence of the Benchers, they would conduct moots which were very stimulating. Overall, my dinner experiences outweighed my private legal studies at home. I gained further political knowledge and experience through my contacts with Singapore MPs who transited through London. A couple of them encouraged me to join the ruling PAP. I remember particularly Mr Joe Conceicao who was our Ambassador to Moscow. He would spend his vacation in London and sure enough, he would contact me as his so-called 'resourceful friend'. I knew him as a lecturer of the Singapore Teachers' Training College.

Member of The Honourable Society of Gray's Inn in London (1980).

Mr Joe Conceicao, Ambassador & MP.

I was nearing the end of my tour of duty. My elder son Tien passed his General Certificate of Education (G.C.E.). I was hoping to get a year's extension for my daughter Gek to complete her G.C.E. level. But my application for extension was disallowed on the grounds of exigencies of service. Meanwhile I received a personal note from Mr S.R.Nathan, who was then the First Permanent Secretary of MFA, explaining why I was chosen for the KL posting. He knew me personally and had full knowledge of my background and language qualifications. It was indeed a blessing from the Lord, as my career star shone brilliantly there. In fact, in celebration of my 80th birthday, my son Tien played a DVD compilation of tributes or accolades from my old colleagues, much to my amazement as he had approached them without my knowledge. Anyway I applied for a month's leave and returned to Singapore via the United States.

Two of my kind colleagues, i.e. Bob in New York Mission, Peter Chan in Washington, put us up in their residences. For the rest of the westbound journey, we travelled by Greyhound Bus. We visited the Niagara Falls, Yellowstone National Park (largest US nature reserve), Grand Canyon in Arizona, Hoover Dam (highest concrete dam in US), Las Vegas in Nevada (we earned 2 gaming certificates), San Francisco and thence by SIA plane to Honolulu, capital of Hawaii. By divine providence, I was awarded in 1989 by the Public Service Commission the "Free Air Passage" which entitled only me to do a round trip to the United States again as my choice. As for my family, I had to pay for their air passages. We did a southern tour of the United States this time.

With Saudi and Brunei diplomats in London.

CHAPTER 10
FOURTH DIPLOMATIC POSTING IN KUALA LUMPUR

I felt a deep sense of fulfilment regarding my London posting. It was by divine providence that my long-held dream of working in London was fulfilled. In hindsight, I felt the same about my continued posting to Kuala Lumpur (KL). The exigency of service as conveyed to me in London arose as a result of the resignation of our Information Officer in KL. By the time I assumed my post on 2 January 1981, my predecessor had migrated to Australia. Nevertheless, he had primed someone working in the tabloid "The Echo". I saw therein a report of my curriculum vitae.

After working in Tokyo, New Delhi and London Missions, this was the first time I was impressed by the beautiful architecture of our very own building situated at 209 Jalan Tun Razak. Next to this was another building for accommodating our junior officers. When High Commissioner Maurice Baker saw me, he was very happy to welcome me, having been primed by Perm Sec S.R.Nathan who was instrumental in getting me posted here. I assured HC Maurice that I would give of my best and even aspired

*With High Commissioner Maurice Baker at SHC, 209 Jalan
Tun Razak, KL. 2 January 1981. The others are
Mr Lim's wife and children.*

*With High Commissioner Maurice Baker at SHC, 209 Jalan
Tun Razak, KL.2 January 1981. The others are
Mr Lim's wife and children.*

to do well for the reputation of our mission. He came across as a "pukka" gentleman, a good listener who showed mutual respect and helpful. It was a great delight to talk with him in private about our perceptions of 'literature is life' and 'love is irrational' as well as political issues and personages. He was very encouraging in his attitude towards my diligent research on Malaysian personalities and my flair for languages. In fact, he was humble enough to consult me occasionally on certain Latin or Malay phrases or proverbs. He commented that I would make a very good teacher.

To facilitate my professional work, he encouraged me to cultivate as many Malaysian contacts as possible and advised me not to worry too much about entertainment expenditure. Moreover, he would pass over some of his invitations to me, which enabled me to come in touch with, for instance, a royal personage. When I met Chief Justice Azlan Shah for the first time, I did not know who he was. I greeted him respectfully with a smile and introduced myself. His first question to me, which was uttered with considerable confidence and dignity, was: *"Where is Maurice?"* I replied humbly: *"He isn't feeling well and has asked me to attend this occasion on his behalf."* Obviously, he knew HC Maurice very well. I told him that I had just been transferred from the High Commission in London and after an exchange of pleasantries, I discovered that he was the Chief Justice of Malaysia. On further research about him, I gathered that he was from the Perak royalty. He later became the Sultan of Perak, i.e. Sultan Azlan Shah as he was popularly known. It was not too difficult to come in contact with Malaysian Ministers. They were politicians who needed to be popular, pleasant and sociable. In this regard, I had ample opportunities to talk with them and got to know them personally. For example, through my various encounters with Datuk

Musa Hitam, who later became the Deputy Prime Minister, I was able to joke with him whenever we met each other, either at official functions or his residence where he was more relaxed and a 'live wire' of the party. In this way, I was able to build up the profiles of different personages apart from newspaper sources. The mission was also ill-equipped with reference books in English or Malay. So I took pains to select useful books of information every weekend from many bookstores in KL. For example, I managed to find Malaysian Civil Service gazettes setting out the careers of senior officers in the government. In this respect, HC commended me for being able to produce urgently the CV of a particular official, which he said the other mission officers were unable to do so.

With full support from HC, I decided to employ a lady Chinese translator in addition to our existing Malay translator of Chinese ethnicity. I encouraged them to consult me if they had any difficulty in translating into good English all the relevant reports or issues of bilateral significance. These translations were circulated to all senior officers including HC. As for me, from the Utusan Melayu (In Jawi, a modified form of Arabic script), I would personally pick out and translate immediately news reports or articles of importance to MFA. My faxes to MFA would also be circulated.

By divine providence, it was around this time that MFA instituted an incentive scheme to encourage foreign service officers to master foreign languages. In my case, I was already eligible for the language allowance and was pleased to receive a monthly payment slip of $150. Not only had I acquired the Cambridge HSC Malay including Jawi but also Standard III, the highest level set by the Civil Service Examination Board. I gathered from HC Low Choon Ming, my former Director of Administration in MFA that no other officer held that Standard III qualification. In fact, to put my flair for Malay and Jawi to the test, I participated in the National Language Public Examination in August 1966 (Individual Awards by Esso Standard Ltd.) and won the second prize.

Among the many Utusan Melayu reports that I had translated and transmitted to MFA was one that roiled MFA upper echelon and the Cabinet. It was Sunday when I saw the Jawi report on the front page of Utusan Melayu. I was quite perturbed during my translation of it, because the reporter mentioned the name of the officer Jeffrey Singham (deceased). According to him, the reporter failed to contact me for comments on a certain rumour about PM LKY. He claimed to know me personally, so Jeffrey spoke to him without mentioning that "it's off the record". As far as the reporter was concerned, it was a 'scoop'. Anyway Jeffrey was able to exculpate himself and got off scot-free with HC's support. The moral of this story is that "too many cooks spoil the broth". It could result in confusion or even leakage of confidential information as it had happened before. For that reason, I was appointed as the official spokesman of the Singapore High Commission. HC's good opinion of me was in his own words: *"He is shrewd"* (i.e. astute).

My experience with Malaysian journalists showed that they were capable of using different tactics to involve me in their reports. If I said that I had no comment to make regarding a certain issue, they would still report me as saying that "First Secretary Mr Lim Chin Leong, official spokesman of the Singapore High Commission, neither confirmed nor denied it". Another sinister tactic by a certain female journalist, who knew me, was to write an article in advance on a sensitive issue like 'supply of water to Singapore' in the context of PAS Youth threatening to cut off water supply to

Singapore. She phoned me to ask me in a friendly manner whether she could check with me certain basic facts, such as the costs and quantum of raw water and treated water as well as the quantity of refined water sold to Johor. I discovered later from her slanted tabloid article in Malay that her intention was to show that she had actually discussed the topic with me, even though our conversation lasted no more than five minutes! You could say it was trickery, but MFA would query how the whole incident had come about.

As a diplomat operating in KL, despite whatever the Malay writers had written about us, it was nevertheless my bounden duty to continue to build up a good rapport with them and even ask them how we could maintain peaceful relations between two very close neighbours. But we should also respect this proverbial view of theirs: *"Mulut tempayan boleh ditutup, tetapi mulut orang, apa boleh buat?"* (The mouth of a jar can be closed, but what can you do with the mouth of people?) In this connection, there was another Malay proverb which I quoted to MFA from time to time in my reports, i.e. *"Ayer tenang, jangan sangka tiada buaya"* (The water is calm,but don't think there is no crocodile). What I meant by this saying was that peaceful relationship with Malaysia could be disrupted by underlying forces from time to time. So I am not surprised by present events in our bilateral relations. The Malay newspapers are mouthpieces of their political masters. Therefore we should be on the qui vive.

Here I would like to relate an interesting anecdote of a protest demonstration at the High Commission's gate. A group from the youth wing of Parti Islam SeMalaysia (PAS) turned up at the gate in order to hand a strong protest note to the government of Singapore. I was instructed to deal with them. I approached them calmly and told them that I could

125

admit only the leader and his deputy to hear them out in the visitors' room. One of them who was bilingual informed me that they wished to meet with the High Commissioner. I replied that he was not available as he had gone out. I casually asked him in English how many of them were present. He turned around to look at the leader of the group. The leader whom I recognised as Mohd Sabu remarked in Malay (English translation): *"Tell Mr Lim that if he thinks we are not big enough, we can call more supporters to come immediately"*. Evidently the leader misinterpreted my intention that I was trying to belittle them. To eschew any argument, I invited Mohd Sabu and his bilingual deputy to have a short meeting with me. I was conscious of the fact that the leaders must be seen to have succeeded in delivering their protest note. This brief meeting was necessary to give due respect to the leaders, thereby defusing the tension. They would feel good. In hindsight, it was the right thing to do, because Mohd Sabu is today the Defence Minister of Malaysia, much to my surprise! I attribute this to divine providence.

It is important to note that during my extraordinarily long tenure of service from January 1981 to March 1991, I observed the growth of Islamic fundamentalism which led to a defensive reassertion of Islamic values and practices among the Muslim Malay ruling elite. I recall the impact of the Iranian Revolution of 1979. Among the PAS leaders, Datuk Abdul Hadi Awang was much influenced by the ideology of Ayatollah Ruhollah Khomeini. He is now the leader of PAS and is intent on establishing the Islamic religious law called 'shariah' at federal level, if possible. I noticed its implementation particularly in Trengganu and Kelantan when I visited the states there. The Malay newspapers played up the supremacy of Muslim Malays. Unlike Singapore, they could raise issues on race, language and religion with impunity.

During this period, I was introduced by a Malay friend to the leader of ABIM (Angkatan Belia Islam Malaysia), a Muslim youth organisation, by the name of Anwar Ibrahim. He was then running a school for Muslim youth. My Malay friend was actually a close associate of Anwar and was helping the latter not only in teaching but also in Muslim welfare activities. I gathered from him that they were watching political events in the Middle East including Israel. Believing in Muslim solidarity, they would participate in protest demonstrations against the US, calling for boycott of US goods etc. Although they had associates in PAS, they eventually joined UMNO. I continued to keep in touch with them through social and official functions, as well as private lunches. To me, Anwar came across as a dynamic and charismatic leader. As a student activist making strident calls for Islamisation and Malay-language education,he was detained under the Internal Security Act (ISA). But in 1982, he was brought into the Mahathir government. He was perceived as an heir apparent to PM Mahathir. But sadly, he was removed from his office of Deputy Prime Minister by PM Mahathir on 2 September 1998.

The last time I met him was in Singapore, after my return to MFA headquarters in 1991, when I accompanied him to see Minister George Yeo at the Ministry. At this meeting, I was impressed by his highbrow interest in opera and mention of the renowned Italian operatic singer Pavarotti. In all my years in Malaysia, I had not heard of any politician who showed such interest. On the contrary, they would criticise western music as decadent, such as pop music. Instead they replaced it with Islamic pop music called 'qasidah'. PAS politicians even talked of discarding TV sets. Deviationist teachings of Islam began to proliferate, e.g. members of Darul Arqam dressed themselves in green robes

Met Mr Anwar Ibrahim in KL in 1986.
He is now PM-in-waiting.

and turbans. Its leader claimed to be the representative of Prophet Muhammad. Some female civil servants declined to shake hands with me.

Curiously enough, as I was nearing the end of my first tour of duty, MFA Director of Administration Mrs Mohideen wrote to HC Maurice that the posting committee decided to send me to Riyadh, capital of Saudi Arabia, to head our mission there, because I could read and speak Arabic. I studied the language with a private Arabic tutor and then in 1962 sat for the Cambridge HSC Examination in Classical Arabic, all at my own expense. Divine providence had guided me to develop a liking for this most difficult language as though I was already destined to use it in my foreign service. Frankly, HC was not too happy about the news and asked me to consult my wife before making my decision to accept or decline it. She was not in favour of it because there were social restrictions imposed on women, e.g. not allowed to drive alone, strict observance of conservative attire, no Catholic church to attend Sunday Mass. I saw HC the next morning and told him of our decision to decline the posting. He remarked with some cheer in his face: *"Of course, I will always be happy to have you around. I am going to write a personal letter to Mrs Mohideen. Please go on the next courier run."* I did as I was told.

When Mrs Mohideen read the letter, she was surprised and commented: *"I thought all along you were interested in a posting to Riyadh."* I revealed the truth to her and she reluctantly agreed. In hindsight, divine providence had in store for me my final posting to Cairo prior to my retirement. For us, it turned out to be a far better choice.

By divine providence, I was invited to a special donors' party organised by the Regional Islamic Council for Asia and the Pacific (RISEAP). Its President was Tunku Abdul

Rahman Putra, founding father (first Prime Minister) of Malaysia. As a student in Kluang, Johor, I had heard of his famous name and the frequent shouts of 'Merdeka!' everywhere; so also in Singapore of our founding father Lee Kuan Yew and the shouts of 'Merdeka' (Independence). In fact, I dreamt of meeting them and shaking their hands. How amazing that divine providence had made it come to pass by the providential change of my career from teaching to foreign service!

Prior to meeting Tunku Abdul Rahman, I had been reading his interesting articles in the English tabloid called 'The Star'. It was marvellous that I was able to have a little chat with him at the donors' party in KL. I have a copy of his letter with the logo of a 4-legged creature with 2 wings and a tail sitting upon the Malay word 'DIBEBASKAN' (i.e. Freed). This is my translation of its Malay content written in refined prose:-

To Donor Mr C.L.Lim,

On behalf of the Regional Islamic Council for Asia and the Pacific (RISEAP), I thank you very much (ribuan terima kasih = thousands of thanks) for your generous donation and purchase of the videotape titled "Book of Signs / Book of Allah" produced by this Council. Your donation will be used to fund the religious projects of this Council.

May God bless your donation.

Yours sincerely,
(Personal signature of Tunku Abdul Rahman Putra)
PRESIDENT

Address: 1 Jalan Tunku, 50480 Kuala Lumpur

Mr. C. L. Lim

Also met him in person at a party for a little chat.

SAUDARA/SAUDARI YANG DERMAWAN,

SAYA BAGI PIHAK MAJLIS DAKWAH ISLAMIAH RANTAU ASIA DAN PASIFIK (RISEAP) MENGUCAPKAN RIBUAN TERIMA KASIH KEPADA SAUDARA/SAUDARI YANG TELAH BERMURAH HATI MENDERMA SAMBIL MEMBELI VIDEO "BOOK OF SIGNS / KITAB ALLAH" TERBITAN MAJLIS INI. DERMA SAUDARA/SAUDARI ITU AKAN DIGUNAKAN BAGI KERJA-KERJA DAKWAH MAJLIS INI.

SEMUGA ALLAH S.W.T. MENGRAHMATI DERMA SAUDARA/SAUDARI ITU, INSYA'ALLAH.

SEKIAN, WASSALAM.

YANG IKHLAS,

(TUNKU ABDUL RAHMAN PUTRA)
PRESIDEN

TUNKU ABDUL RAHMAN PUTRA AL-HAJ (DMN, CH.)
16. Jalan Tunku Abdul Rahman, 10350 Pulau Pinang. Tal. 374876
1. Jalan Tunku, 50480 Kuala Lumpur. Tal. 2983914

Letter of gratitude to Mr Lim from Tunku Abdul Rahman as President of RISEAP. (NB: He was the 1st Prime Minister of Malaysia.)

The oft-repeated Malay word 'dakwah' is derived from Arabic and means 'propagation' of the faith (Islam). This word has positive implications and is therefore often used in Malay newspapers and magazines. At the same time, it is also exploited by deviationists of Islam (penyelewengan) for their own purposes.

Following the above event was another unexpected and somewhat sudden event. Nobody in the mission told me or even hinted that the President of Singapore was making a private visit to the mission. As usual I was poring over my Malay newspapers. My door was open and then I heard a gentle knock. I looked up and was surprised to see HC Maurice, thinking that he needed urgent assistance. Then he said rather mysteriously: *"You have a visitor."* Thereupon President Devan Nair appeared at the doorway, much to my astonishment. HC discreetly stood outside while President Devan was having a little chat with me. He revealed that he was going for a holiday in Pangkor Island (near Teluk Anson in Perak). Since I knew him personally, HC proposed that I accompany him using our mission's transport while the President travelled in his own car accompanied by his aides. In Pangkor I overheard his aides wondering how I got to know the President. I made it a point not to reveal our personal relationship. In 1981, he became the third President of Singapore when I was posted to KL from London. In Chapter 9, I have disclosed how I forged my personal relationship with him. Here I would like to add more information about him, which I had gleaned from our tete-a-tetes. As a contemporary, I admired his fortitude in his anti-colonial activities resulting in his detention on St John's Island. There he immersed himself in books and dubbed the island as his 'St John's University'. There he met anti-colonial lawyer Lee Kuan Yew. Later he became one of the convenors of PAP's founding in 1954. I recall that he had many friends and supporters in KL and was the only candidate who won a Malaysian Parliamentary constituency under the banner of Democratic Action Party (DAP). But sadly, he eventually fell out with LKY over the issue of alcoholism and its concomitant political problem. As the official spokesman of the Singapore High Commission, I was involved in clarifying the position of the Singapore Government in the New Straits Times (Malaysia) in response to Mr Devan Nair's non-acrimonious letter published by the newspaper. My good relationship with the editorial staff helped in getting all our official replies published as soon as possible.

OCTOBER 6, 1987   NST

the Editor

Devan Nair: I am no alcoholic

... and why I rejected the conditional pension

I REFER to the letter from Mr Lim Chin Leong, First Secretary of the Singapore High Commission (NST, Sept 30), in response to one of your correspondents, which was brought to my attention only on Oct 3. The First Secretary correctly restated Mr Lee Kuan Yew's position as given in the Far Eastern Economic Review (Feb 5). I had accepted this as Mr Lee's position, although I do not agree with it.

I do not have a High Commission in Kuala Lumpur to represent me, and it is my relatives and my friends and well-wishers in Malaysia, to personally restate my own position. I hope they understand that a restatement of position is by no means a re-opening of dispute with the Singapore Government, or any disagreement. I don't... it would be improper to choose the columns of a newspaper in a friendly neighbouring country for the purpose.

As far as I can make out, Mr Lee and I are agreed to disagree. There is no need for anybody to get embroiled over my disagreement. Nobody in Singapore has.

Now for my restatement. Seven physicians in Singapore did indeed make the diagnosis of alcoholism. They had great difficulty in... my judgment as... to me that the doctors had told him that the impairment to my judgment and perception could not be repaired. It was Dr Stanley Gitlow, a clinical professor of medicine in New York,

who established, after conclusive tests, which I had insisted upon, that there was nothing to repair.

Not every straw in the wind is grist for the mill, and I dislike bandying Dr Gitlow's distinguished name in public. I respect him too much for that. In any case, that I can state here is that I took the precaution of calling on Dr Gitlow in New York before I returned to Singapore in May this year, in order to acquaint him with my present position. I may also add that Dr Gitlow was not asked to second any conclusion I had made no pre-diagnosed in Singapore. He had no difficulty accepting the pre-diagnosis, and for a very good reason. The patient himself had subscribed to it then.

In my letter to the Far Eastern Economic Review of Feb 5, I explained why I... the fact accept the monicker of alcoholism, for years, despite the welcomed assurances on this score from qualified medical circles in the United States.

There is nothing to argue about. Mr Lee accepts my position that I was never an alcoholic, and will act in future on the assumption that I was never an alcoholic, for my part, I do not accept or discards the diagnosis of alcoholism made by seven Singapore doctors. That

is his privilege. They were proved wrong about the brain damage, in any case.

I did not reject the pension of 16,000 per month, God knows, and my wife and I certainly do, that I could have done with retirement provisions after nearly three years, and... their insignificant public service. What did reject were the conditions which went along with it. This was how I put it in my letter to the Far Eastern Economic Review:

"It will now be clear to everyone why my family and I will never accept the conditional pension approved by the... a pensioned... maybe, condition when compared to a pensioned... condition in a cage, in which I would have been legislatively locked up forever in a mis-diagnosis. Dr Gitlow never expected such an outcome. I know he was shocked.

"It will now be clear to everyone why my family and I will never accept the conditional pension... that I should spend the remainder of my days in sackcloth and ashes, in what would be tantamount to the psychiatric ward of a Singapore version of the Gulag, closely monitored and supervised by keepers of sackcloth, maybe, considering that a pensionless retirement in Singapore will certainly impose on my wife and me the need for a very bare existence — but without ashes."

The First Secretary to the Singapore High Commission now says that this conditional pension moved in Parliament "was based on the compassionate assumption that Mr Nair needed help including medical help." Congratulations to Orwellian Newspeak! could not have

been some other medical cause to explain the acute confusion that I was in, I simply cannot recognise myself in the reports of bizarre conduct which came down to me. Although I had been assured that I had committed no crime, nor divulged any secret of State, it was nonetheless a condition which was surely unbecoming of a Head of State. I therefore have no regret that I, in my letter published in The Straits Times (Sept 4, 1980), I had humbly apologised to the people of Singapore. That apology still stands, without qualification or reservation of any kind.

The position I took in my final letter on the subject to take attention. It was been brief reiteration. I was and am aware that Mr Lee unreservedly withdrew the offending statement he made in his letter to me of April 22, 1985, about my parents, brothers, uncles and sisters. I seek nothing more.

For the rest — and the pension be blowed — my own perception and knowledge of myself, as I have of persuading him to change his opinion. Wisely, neither of us have tried to do so. So let it remain. No hard feelings, certainly we on my side. One does not deprive a sense of liberation. May I appeal to your student, whether critics or supporters, will now allow Mr Lee and me to go our separate ways?

C.V. DEVAN NAIR
Singapore

NST Letters from Mr Lim and Mr Devan Nair.

Page 9
30-9-87

NEW STRAITS TIMES, WEDNESDAY,

Letters

Kuan Yew did not agree that doctors were wrong

VOX POPULI, Vox Dei's letter of Sept 17 said that Mr Lee Kuan Yew had through his Press Secretary James Fu retracted offending sentences about Mr Devan Nair "unreservedly and stands corrected for the future".

Mr Lee does not stand corrected over the diagnosis of a panel of seven physicians in Singapore that Mr Nair was an alcoholic. The diagnosis was confirmed by an American specialist, a clinical professor of medicine in New York, Dr Stanley Gitlow.

What James Fu wrote to the *Far Eastern Economic Review* of Feb 21 was:

"Now Mr Nair has concluded that he never suffered from alcoholism. He wrote that 'the diagnosis of alcoholism no longer holds water', and that when he was sent to Pennsylvania for treatment, it was 'for a non-existent condition, as it now transpires'. Mr Lee accepts this as his position, and will act on this assumption in future."

It means that Mr Lee accepts that Mr Nair's position was that he was never an alcoholic, and that Mr Lee will in future act on this assumption. It does not mean that Mr Lee agreed with Mr Nair that the seven Singapore doctors and the American specialist were all wrong in their diagnosis.

The pension for $5,000 per month for Mr Nair was moved in Parliament by the Minister for Law, Mr E.W. Barker. It was based on the compassionate assumption that Mr Nair needed help, including medical help. He turned it down. This is his privilege.

LIM CHIN LEONG
First Secretary
Singapore High
Commission

PRIVATE & CONFIDENTIAL

Private comment :-
Devan Nair is a personal friend of mine though very few know about it; not even Maurice Baker, my H.C. in KL. The latter was probably surprised when Devan asked to see me in my office. I myself was surprised when he popped into my office and had a little chat with me. Obviously he did not forget me when he was President on a visit to KL. Maurice asked me to accompany him on his visit to Pulau Pangkor (Perak). I overheard his aides wondering how I got to know him. I did not reveal.

NST Letters from Mr Lim and Mr Devan Nair.

Two big issues that attracted the attention of the local press was the 'Marxist conspiracy' and 'liberation theology'. When these issues first surfaced in the local press, the perceptions of those opposed to the Singapore Government here were negative and provocative. This was quite clear from the letters published by the local press, which gave the impression of a concerted attack against the government of Singapore. As a consequence, I had a lot on my plate, having to rebut or refute all the allegations. The arrest of some Catholics including the warning to Archbishop Gregory Yong in Singapore riled the Catholic community here including my brother-in-law Father Paul Tan, who later became the Bishop for Johor and Melaka (Malacca). I remember the Archbishop in KL commenting on his character. He said that as a Jesuit, he was prepared to "die for his beliefs". I had a tête-à-tête with him with the view to getting him to refrain from writing confrontational letters to the New Straits Times. I emphasised to him the greater importance of peaceful, harmonious, familial relations than his somewhat disruptive, controversial letters to the press. My report to MFA surprisingly evoked a personal response from Minister S.Rajaratnam who wrote to me directly informing me that he had written to Father Paul but was disappointed that he did not receive the courtesy of a reply. Be that as it may, their controversial correspondence in the press ceased thereafter.

As a member of the Society of Jesus, Father Paul Tan believed strongly in social justice. As a response to 'Marxist conspiracy', he published a small booklet to explain the origin of 'liberation theology' and its goals. The Jesuits are renowned for their great learning, fortitude, personal sacrifice and sworn to obedience, celibacy and poverty. This evokes two incidents in his life, which he narrated to me.

With Bishop Paul Tan, brother-in-law of Mr Lim, i/c diocese of Johor & Melaka. The others are his close relations.

Bishop Paul Tan is now retired in Plentong, Johor Bahru.

He was posted as a priest to a Latin American country. One evening, a couple of rogues attempted to rob the church, but when they were told that the Chinese priest, who was in the church, was a kung fu fighter, they beat a hasty retreat. Actually he was nervous but did not show it!

After his service in Latin America, he went to Europe where he eventually served the 'general' (i.e. head of his religious order) in the Vatican in Rome. By divine providence, after many years, we met each other in KL where my wife, his older sister, rendered assistance in the library of the Catholic Centre which he had set up. It was after my return to Singapore in 1991 that I heard of his dreadful car accident and had to be taken to a hospital in Malacca for emergency treatment. After his miraculous recovery, I had occasion to learn something from his dire experience. The first question I asked him was what he uttered when he met with the accident. He said: *"Lord, have mercy on me."* Then he passed out. Divine providence had prolonged his life to fulfil the need of the Church for more priests like him. He is now retired as Bishop Emeritus in Plentong, Johor Bahru.

After my promotion as First Secretary, I decided to change my old Japanese car to a Mercedes-Benz, as my children were growing bigger. One evening, my wife and I attended a dinner party at the residence of the First Secretary of the Indian High Commission. I had parked my car at the roadside near his residence. After the party, I walked out to look for my car, but I could not find it, much to my consternation. After checking by walking up and down the road, I began to feel sure that it had been stolen. The next morning I made a police report. As it was a diplomatic car, the matter was handled by a senior officer of the police headquarters in KL. By divine providence, the car was recovered on the thirteenth day after a period of considerable anxiety and fervent prayers to the Lord. Only the Mercedes emblem on the bonnet was removed when I went to the police station to collect my car. The inspector pointed out the thief and commented that he was a notorious thief who had been in and out of prison several times.

Within the same year, our office station wagon was stolen. Our driver parked the vehicle at a shop in Bangsar and forgot to lock it. When he came out of the shop, he was stunned to find it missing. But by divine providence, it was recovered after a week. I did not sack the driver for his forgetfulness. As the saying goes: *"To err is human; to forgive is divine."*

In London, it was by divine providence that I was able to attend for the first time parliamentary sessions in the famous Houses of Parliament. In KL, I had many opportunities to attend not only sessions in the Malaysian Parliament but also the UMNO General Assemblies, which were all conducted in Malay (Bahasa Malaysia). Incidentally, in one of the visits by our parliamentary delegation, I came across two familiar faces, viz. Mr Chiam See Tong, Dr Tan Cheng Bock. I have written about Mr Chiam in Chapter 7 and I wonder how many people know about this part of his life. I was surprised to meet him, being the only opposition MP in the delegation. He approached me with a smile and asked me for some clarification of the programme of visit. As I had some personal reservations in speaking with him in the presence of the PAP MPs, I turned my attention to Dr Tan Cheng Bock. I recall talking to Dr Tan while he was doing some repairs at the drain in front of his house, which faced my sister-in-law's house. He will remember Mrs Clara Chan residing at No. 1, Faber Green. He asked me for my opinion on the issue of Nominated MPs. At that time, I was of the view that it was not appropriate or infra dig for opposition candidates to be nominated by the PAP government. They should fight to win and not enter Parliament by this means.

The exciting aspect of my occupation was to keep a constant watch on the political dynamics in Malaysia. By the beginning of 1987, it was clear to me that a faction in UMNO led by Tengku Razaleigh Hamzah endeavoured to topple PM Mahathir. I remember that Tengku Razaleigh failed in his attempt, because Mahathir won narrowly by 43 votes in the party leadership elections. There was a lot of discontent or disaffection due to PM Mahathir's style of authoritarian governance or dictatorship as some like Tunku Abdul Rahman would prefer to call it. As a result, there was a groundswell of opposition to his rule. He was perceived to be arrogating to himself the executive and judicial powers. In fact, he sacked Tun Salleh Abas with whom I was acquainted. He was Lord President of the Supreme Court, the highest judge in the land. I regarded him as a courageous judge who acted independently of the other branches of government. He said that he was extremely humiliated so much so that he wanted to get away from it all by being a farmer!

PM Mahathir was also then Home Affairs Minister, having previously removed his political comrade Datuk Musa Hitam from that post. On the grounds of national security, he ordered the staggered arrest of 119 prominent politicians from different parties including UMNO, trade unionists, educators, community leaders and outspoken critics of the government. I also heard that Mr Lee Kim Sai, an outspoken leader of the Malaysian Chinese Association (MCA), a component party of the ruling coalition, was tipped off and escaped to Australia. Father Paul Tan had his bag packed ready, waiting to be arrested. But by the grace of God, nothing happened to him. This whole event was known as 'operation lalang' (lalang is Malay for weed). In the same year, the old UMNO was declared as an 'unlawful society' and Mahathir formed a new UMNO called 'UMNO BARU'. The next year, Tengku Razaleigh formed Semangat '46 as a revival of the spirit of 1946 when the original UMNO was founded by Dato' Onn Jaafar in Johor.

As if the above crises were not enough, Mahathir faced further challenges from a couple of sultans in peninsular Malaysia. It was an open secret that he intended to institute a Constitutional Court in order to curb the behaviour of the sultans. He managed to get it passed through Parliament. I also heard the canard that the Sultan of Johor would shoot him with his pistol if Mahathir dared to hold a political rally in Johor. As it turned out, it proved to be false.

Nevertheless I do not doubt the Sultan's temperament to take action if he really felt strongly about it. When I was a teacher and a Johor national in 1957, I met him by chance at the Hong Kong Restaurant in Johor Bahru, where I was introduced to him by a lawyer-friend as the 'Raja Muda' (Crown Prince). He narrated quite proudly how he pursued in his helicopter a robber who was escaping in his speedboat in the Straits of Johor. Aiming his pistol at the robber, he shot him dead. By divine providence, I met him again in August 1985 when I accompanied our parliamentary delegation to Johor Bahru as the secretary. He was then Sultan Iskandar concurrently Yang di-Pertuan Agong (Paramount Ruler). I have a Straits Times photo dated 24 August 1985 presented by Chief Editor Mr Peter Lim, which showed me and three others listening to him. He hosted a dinner for us.

Just before finishing the dinner, he approached me, seeming to recognise me and sensing his good mood, I took the opportunity to ask him a few questions by way of conversation. In this situation, I had the advantage of sitting at the end of the long table. The Sultan was quite candid in his response to my questions.

Sultan Iskandar of Johor concurrently Yang Di-Pertuan Agong of Malaysia. Extract from Straits Times of 24 August 1985. Presented by Chief Editor Peter Lim.

Chance to converse with Sultan Iskandar of Johor, who was also then King of Malaysia in August 1985.

I have no doubt that the aforementioned crises would have caused PM Mahathir tremendous stress. I recall that in January 1989, Mahathir was finally warded in hospital for a heart bypass operation. Prior to that, some time was spent in deciding whether to fly him to the US for the surgery or get it done in KL, because he was critically ill. He decided to have it done in the hospital here and told the heart specialist Dr Yahya Awang to operate on him. Yahya was assisted by a team of surgeons. One of the American surgeons joked with him: *"You'd better ask for medical asylum in the US."* Mahathir's family prayed fervently for him. By the grace of God, he had a miraculous recovery and live till now to tell the world that "if not for the heart-lung machine, he would have died."

I also learnt that on the night when he experienced angina, he did not call for an ambulance but instead drove to the hospital in his car. Then he struggled to walk up the staircase to the cardiologist's clinic. Fortunately for him, the hospital had only the drug streptokinase to save him. My reports to MFA evoked an offer of assistance from Singapore, but Mahathir declined. But at least he would remember our gesture of goodwill and concern.

Another event in my life shows how divine providence acts in mysterious ways. I did not know that several of our citizens who climbed Mount Berlumut were lost in the jungles until our mission received a message from MFA requesting assistance as a result of phone calls from worried and anxious parents in Singapore. HC Nathan, who had succeeded HC Maurice, asked me to go to Kluang and render assistance in whatever way I could. The mountain is located within the district of Kluang, my birthplace as the reader may recall. To me, it was amazing that the MP for Kluang was none other than the son of my aunt, my benefactress when I was in St Andrew's School in 1955. He introduced me to the Chief Police Officer (CPO). With their cooperation, the search-and-rescue operation was expedited. Within a week, all the 'lost ones' were rescued. The news spread like wildfire and I became the centre of media attention. The Singapore media interviewed me and then the climbers. As expected, all this publicity was carried over the TV and in the press. When I returned immediately to KL, a Malay cameraman from RTM (Radio Television Malaysia) approached me to say a few words in Malay about the incident. Knowing the Malaysian media, I was careful to say the right things, not forgetting to express our government's appreciation for all the cooperation and help rendered to us. Except from the newspapers, I never saw the TV version nor heard the radio broadcast of the incident. But some kind friends from MFA Singapore and KL either phoned or wrote to me to congratulate me, saying such things as: *"I saw you on TV. You are great, man. You are a hero to me. You said the right things."* In hindsight, all my deeds were performed extempore. In many situations, I had to think on my feet.

As a firm believer in divine providence, I perceive the three High Commissioners in KL Mission as 'instruments of God', viz. Mr Maurice Baker, Mr S.R.Nathan, Mr Low Choon Ming. They could see through my potential and helped me to fulfil it. HC Maurice gave me many opportunities to meet personages in formal functions, such as the then Crown Prince Akihito of Japan and Prince Sihanouk of Cambodia. Both of them emphasised the excellent bilateral relations. The way Prince Akihito spoke English to me sounded like a rehearsed speech. Prince Sihanouk spoke to me in a perceptibly humble manner, expressing repeatedly his gratitude for Singapore's assistance. Their personal speeches to me gave me the impression that Singapore had done right to earn their respect or gratitude.

I also met DPM Goh Keng Swee again in KL. HC Maurice informed me that he was coming to stay in KL for a night. There was no problem with his hotel accommodation except his dinner at the hotel, which had already been arranged. Unexpectedly, at the last moment, he asked HC Maurice to take him to an Indian stall to enjoy his favourite mutton soup!

His asthmatic condition was a concern. I had seen him suffer from a serious bout in hospital in KL. At his request on various occasions, I had stood in for him. On my 80th birthday (25-6-2016), I learnt from my elder son Tien that Mr Maurice Baker had Parkinson's. Tien wanted to surprise me by trying to invite my former kind HCs and colleagues who had served with me in KL and Mr Peter Ho Hak Ean (now Sr. Adviser, Centre for Strategic Futures, PM's Office), who was kind and helpful to me when I was in MFA HQ. Tien compiled a memorable DVD record of their tributes to me. I also learnt from Tien that Mr Nathan was undergoing dialysis in the Singapore General Hospital. Mr Maurice passed away on 11 July 2017 at the age of 97 and Mr Nathan on 22 August 2016 at the age of 92.

Here I wish to place on record my prayers for their souls to rest in peace. RIP (Latin: Requiescat in pace).

In Chapter 9, I have written something about Mr Nathan. For the first time, divine providence had emplaced me in KL to work very closely with him. Knowing my character, he had taken me into his confidence. Whatever I learnt from my sources, I would share my confidences with him. As far as I was concerned, he was kind and empathetic towards me whereas other officers gave him the epithets of being a 'task-master' or 'slave-driver'. He was aware of it and explained to me why it was necessary to enforce discipline and diligence, otherwise he would be unable to carry out the mandate of PM LKY to shape up MFA or PM would disband it. That was why he was transferred from the Ministry of Defence where he was the Director of Security and Intelligence to MFA as First Permanent Secretary. I recall that after reading one of my reports to MFA, he wrote me a personal note requesting me to see him during the next courier run. After a closed-door session with him, I emerged feeling inspired by his encouraging words of advice.

Believing in camaraderie and esprit de corps, he would gather us for lunches from time to time. The other officers told me that during these occasions, they felt a great sense of relief and relaxation as I was able to engage Mr Nathan's attention by regaling him with a variety of stories and happenings in Malaysia. During his tenure, I was awarded by the Public Service Commission in 1989 a free air passage sponsored by SIA. I learnt later that I was the last recipient of the award before it was terminated. Anyway, it was a pleasant surprise.

When I first heard of his posting to KL, I had my misgiving, mainly because of his known intelligence background and the actions he had taken against journalists who wrote anti-Singapore articles for the Far Eastern Economic Review, e.g. Ho Kwon Ping who was highly critical of the PAP and eventually jailed under the ISA. He is the son of our former Ambassador to Thailand, whom I met by chance in our Embassy in Tokyo in 1969. Interestingly he is now the Chairman of the Singapore Management University. When Mr Nathan was appointed Executive Chairman of the Straits Times Press, the journalists protested by wearing black armbands to no avail. All these events were observed by Malaysian journalists and the Special Branch in KL.

Unlike HC Maurice, HC Nathan was very active in attending all functions. I continued to be his 'eyes and ears'. I would bring directly to his attention all the relevant reports. Negative messages about him appeared mainly in the tabloids. As far as I was concerned, I made it clear to a couple of journalists that I began my career as a teacher and was seconded to MFA which posted me here to maintain good bilateral relations. Some of them wondered why I had been kept in KL for so long. My usual response was because of my expertise in Malay and Jawi. I learnt that the powers that be in KL were 'uncomfortable' with HC Nathan. Therefore he was transferred to be our Ambassador to Washington, after having served in KL from April 1988 to July 1990. Before he left, he wrote a tribute for all my hard work and helpfulness. He also offered to help me in any way he could. As I was desirous of a change of posting, after having served a decade in KL, I asked a favour of him to get me posted out. True to his promise, I was posted back to headquarters after a further delay of 8 months.

He was succeeded by Mr Low Choon Ming with whom I was first acquainted in New Delhi Mission. Our paths crossed again in London where our families became closer, and finally in KL. A couple of officers in the mission knew that he was my friend. If he had his way, he would certainly like me to continue my tour of duty in KL. Anyway, he was appreciative of my help and camaraderie. We still keep in touch as good friends.

In March 1991, it was time to bid farewell and he did me the honour of hosting an official farewell party at the premises of our High Commission. It was a memorable occasion for me, because the chief editor of New Straits Times (NST) had quietly assigned a familiar reporter to interview me on the spot. I was pleasantly surprised to see a news report dated 18-3-1991 with a coloured photo of me and my successor Mr Jimmy Chua, entitled "Bidding a diplomat adieu". Here below is my very brief selection of the encomiastic expressions used:-

1. Well-known and amiable character in diplomatic circles

2. About 150 foreign diplomats and his personal contacts attended to pay tribute or simply say goodbye to Mr Lim

3. Affectionately known as "almost a permanent fixture" in Malaysia after a 10-year posting here

Mr Lim seeing off a friend. To his left is his happy successor, Jimmy Chua.

Bidding a diplomat adieu NST 18·3·91

IT was a night to bid farewell to a well-known and amiable character in diplomatic circles — Singapore High Commission's First Secretary, Mr Lim Chin Leong.

About 150 foreign diplomats and his personal contacts attended the reception, held at the High Commission along Jalan Tun Razak, to pay tribute or to simply say goodbye to Mr Lim.

Affectionately known as "almost a permanent fixture" in Malaysia, he is returning to his homeland after a 10-year posting here.

He will, however, still be in the foreign service back home.

All through the night, Mr Lim was busy chatting with people, whom he had befriended during his stay here and introducing his successor, Mr Jimmy Chua.

The guests dined on a buffet that included local specialties like *rojak, keoy teow* and continental food.

□ THE Saudi Arabia-Malaysian Friendship Society, set up to strengthen the relationship between the two countries through social, economic and political activities, was launched at the Regent Hotel here on Friday.

The society, which will also organise cultural, educational, sports and social activities, was registered with the Registrar of Societies last month.

Among the objectives of the society are to establish and develop contacts with Malaysian public organisations and individuals working for peace and friendship.

The society will go on a membership drive soon and is presently printing membership forms.

Former Malaysian Ambassador to Saudi Arabia Datuk Mokhtar Ahmad who was appointed president of the society will be the first to lead a team of businessmen to Saudi Arabia under the society next week.

Deputy Public Enterprises Minister Datin Dr Siti Zaharah Sulaiman is a member in the society's advisory panel while the patron is Saudi Arabian Ambassador to Malaysia Mohamad Hassan Wali.

Farewell to Mr Lim by New Straits Times:
New Straits Times dated 18-3-1991 & 19-3-1991.

NEW STRAITS TIMES TUESDAY, MARCH 19, 1991 **7**

Mr Lim's astounding Jawi feat earns him high marks

FOR anyone to have resumed using a language after a 20-year lapse is in itself a noteworthy feat. But if that person had initially mastered the language after only a year, it would be simply remarkable.

Not too many people can claim to have done that.

One who can, however, is the departing Singapore High Commission's First Secretary Lim Chin Leong, who not only achieved that feat, but has done it with Jawi.

Since his posting to Malaysia in 1981, he has been reading *Utusan Melayu* and Sunday's *Utusan Zaman* daily as part of his work to keep up with all the news.

Last Friday, the 54-year-old Mr Lim bade farewell to the friends and contacts he has made during his 10-year tenure as one of the top three diplomats in the Singapore High Commission.

His position will be filled by 34-year-old Jimmy Chua — whose insistence that the focus and attention should be on his predecessor and not him, showed the respect and affection that Mr Lim commands.

Mr Lim is returning to Singapore after more than 13 years of continuous service in the diplomatic corp. He had been given a "cross posting" to Kuala Lumpur direct from London.

His distinguished list of postings include New Delhi and Tokyo, the latter being his first in 1968.

As to his amazing ability to retain his mastery of Jawi, he said: "I have a very retentive memory. But initially when I started in Kuala Lumpur, it was a bit difficult remembering certain fundamentals of the language.

"I find it especially difficult to read those words which have been directly translated from English, but after a while, I eventually figured it out."

He had taken Jawi as an A-level subject, in which a pass was a compulsory requirement for the certificate.

After that, he had little opportunity to use the language, working as a teacher for 10 years before joining the foreign service.

As to why he had done so, he explained: "At that time, most of those in the foreign service were leaving after only one posting and there were a lot of vacancies.

"The Government allowed me to keep my teacher's salary (which was higher), so I felt it would be a good prospect."

Born in Kluang, Johor, Mr Lim, who later 'migrated' to Singapore in 1954, was also the only Chinese student in a Malay language class during his O-levels, and the only one to obtain a credit for it.

"We were given a choice in Standard Nine whether to take Chinese or Malay and my father advised me to choose the latter, which he said was important in this country," he said.

During his 10 years here, Mr Lim has been light-heartedly referred to as a "permanent fixture" and an "institution" in Malaysia because of his length of service, which stretched over three Singapore High Commissioners and two Malaysian Prime Ministers.

"Some of the top men whom I knew from the early days here, have since retired. The most prominent person who has not, would be the Prime Minister (Datuk Seri Dr Mahathir Mohamad)," he added.

He is, however, happy to leave and return home to Singapore. The thing he might miss though, is the food here in Kuala Lumpur, which he claimed to have tried thoroughly.

"But if I crave for them, Malaysia is, after all, only a short step away."

Departing Singapore First Secretary Lim Chin Leong in an expressive mood.

New Straits Times 19-3-1991 "Mr Lim's astounding Jawi feat earns him high marks"

I was further surprised to see an article about me in the NST of 19-3-1991. It was entitled "Mr Lim's astounding Jawi feat earns him high marks". Here below is my extract of the paragraphs among others:-

1. For anyone to have resumed using a language after a 20-year lapse is in itself a noteworthy feat. But if that person had initially mastered the language after only a year, it would be simply remarkable.

2. Not too many people can claim to do that. One who can, however, is the departing Singapore High Commission's First Secretary Lim Chin Leong, who not only achieved that feat, but has done it with Jawi.

3. Since his posting to Malaysia in 1981, he has been reading Utusan Melayu and Sunday's Utusan Zaman daily.

4. He has been given a 'cross posting' to KL direct from London. His distinguished list of postings include New Delhi and Tokyo, the latter being his first in 1968.

5. As to his amazing ability to retain his mastery of Jawi, he said: *"I have a very retentive memory."* * * *

6. He had taken Jawi as an A-level subject in which a pass was a compulsory requirement for the Certificate.

7. Born in Kluang, Johor, Mr Lim, who later migrated to Singapore in 1954, was the only Chinese student in a Malay language class during his O-levels and the only one to obtain a credit for it.

8. We were given a choice in Standard Nine whether to take Chinese or Malay and my father advised me to choose the latter, which he said was important in this country.

9. Mr Lim has been light-heartedly referred to as a "permanent fixture" and an "institution" in Malaysia because of his length of service, which stretched over 3 Singapore High Commissioners and 2 Malaysian Prime Ministers.

10. Some of the top men whom I knew from the early days here have since retired. The most prominent person who has not, would be the Prime Minister (Datuk Seri Dr Mahathir Mohamad).

N.B. Coloured photo below the article shows me "in an expressive mood".

If reader is interested in viewing the press cuttings, letters, photos, video tributes or accolades, books mentioned in this chapter or elsewhere, they are available at the National Archives of Singapore to which I have donated all of them including a Sony globe trotter for receiving world news.

'This is as I see it...' Datuk Seri Dr Mahathir seems to be saying when announcing new Cabinet yesterday. He is flanked by Datuk Musa Hitam on his (right) and Chief Secretary to the Government Tan Sri Sallehuddin. New Sunday Times picture by ABDUL RAHMAN HASHIM

NST 14.7.84

To hear first-hand PM Mahathir's Cabinet announcement. Next to him is Datuk Musa Hitam his right-hand man then. (July 1984).

Group family photo with Mr & Mrs Nathan at Rumah Temasek, KL.

National Day group photo of SHC staff & their families. Mr Lim is behind HC Nathan. Mrs Lim in white cheongsam while daughter Gek in red is 2nd from left in the front row.

With High Commissioner S.R. Nathan from 1988 - 1990.

Rescue of Missing Singapore Hikers in Gunung Berlumut in Kluang (January 1990)

First Secretary Lim Chin Leong was sent to Kluang (his birthplace) to render assistance in cooperation with the authorities there. His meeting with all the rescued hikers was televised in Malaysia & Singapore and widely reported.

```
Mr Lim Chin Leong
KL Mission


Dear Chin Leong


      Attached letter was folded in such
a way that I was unable to see your name
on receipt.


      Letter was therefore inadvertently opened
by me. Apologies for this.


      Saw you on TV regarding missing hikers
at Belumut. You were great!


      Regards.




ANTHONY LIM
MFA (Registry Supervisor)
15 Jan 90
```
Note: This was one of the high dramatic moments in my K.L. posting. My cousin, William Quah, MCA M.P. in Kluang, assisted by getting me in contact with C.P.O. of Kluang Police Station. By the by, I was born in Kluang on 25.6.1936, at X-3 Jalan Morsing! Lim

THE STRAITS TIMES, SATURDAY, JANUARY 6, 1990

HOME

10-day ordeal of the Gr

Five tell story of leeches tigers and raft that caps

By Leong Chan Teik
in Kluang, Johor

LOGGERS at Kejora, some 40 km south-west of Gunung Belumut, were astonished as five weary hikers — their legs blotched by blood-sucking leeches — stumbled into their lumber yard at 1.30 pm yesterday.

The three Singaporean and two Johorean trekkers, who had been missing in the mountainous terrain for 10 days, were immensely relieved to see them.

They were quickly given food and drinks. Mr Lua Lin Chong, 60, the managing director of a sawmill, contacted Kluang police at 2 pm.

That signalled the end of a massive rescue operation involving more than 100 men for the hikers, who have been lost since Dec 26 after scaling the 1,000-metre-high Gunung Belumut.

Later that day, the five were driven to Kluang police station for a tearful but happy reunion with members of their families.

"I've been waiting for you," cried Mr David Hui, 23, as he grew his arms around his sister ai Yuet, one of the Singaporean hikers.

"I'm sorry, I'm sorry," the 29-year-old horticulturist uttered, tears streaming down her face. But apart from the red blotches left by leeches on their legs, the five appeared no worse.

Mr Tan Aik Hwee, 35, whose brother Aik Kee, a 28-year-old production planner was among the missing Singaporeans, summed up the feeling: "The past few nights we haven't been able to sleep. Tonight will be even worse. But it's because we're celebrating!"

Mr Hui, a mechanic, who has been here to monitor rescue efforts since Tuesday, said: "Lai Yuet is so talkative. But that's a good sign."

But Johorean Suhaimi Hasim, 27, and Suri Mohamed Noor, 19, later suffered leg and stomach cramps during a check-up at the hospital here.

Mr Tan Aik Hwee had at 3.15 pm first heard the news that the hikers had been found at Kejora.
He was entering his hotel ...

Mr Lim Chin Leong, the First Secretary of the Singapore High Commission in Kuala Lumpur, thankin chief DSP Abdul Hamid Haji Mohd Noor, with the five hikers looking on: (from left) Tan Aik Kee, I Noor, Norman Shah Kassim and Suhaimi Hasim. Picture by AZIZ HUSSIN.

Hikers showed up here at 1.30 pm

Kg Gajah — Gunung Belumut
Kluang — Air Hitam — Kejora
MALAYSIA
Johor — Kota Tinggi
Straits of Malacca — Johor Baru
SINGAPORE

42, talking excitedly on the phone. "He screamed at me when I entered: 'They have been found!'" Mr Tan recalled.

Mr Lim Chin Leong, the First Secretary of the Singapore High Commission in Kuala Lumpur, who was also here, had called the Tan family when he heard the news.

The hikers poured out their story. They were bitten by sandflies and leeches. The thorns of rattan leaves spiked them.

But through it all, they told each other not to give up hope of leaving the forest safely.

Envoy Nathan thanks Malaysian authorities

THE Singapore High Commission yesterday thanked the Malaysian authorities and those involved in the search for the three Singaporean and two Malaysian hikers who had been missing since Boxing Day.

Singapore's High Commissioner to Malaysia, Mr S. R. Nathan, told Bernama that it was a great relief to all that the five had been found.

"I sincerely thank the Chief Police Officer of Johor and the OCPD of Kluang, and many others who tirelessly continued the search," he said.

and rattan seeds — when they could find them.

But they were lucky not to have ended up as food for tigers.

Mr Norman Shah Kassim, 35, a foreman and the other Singaporean hiker, said: "I saw a few tigers. They were only 10 to 20 metres from us. Luckily they didn't attack us."

They soon lost track of time and threw away clothing and other belongings to lighten their load. Some of these were later picked up by rescuers.

Once, they nearly died when a makeshift raft they were on cap-

infested swamps. Miss Hui said: "I was wearing a pair of shorts, and the leeches came up my thigh and body. Sometimes you could see three or four of them sucking at one spot."

On two days, they heard the whirr of helicopters. "It was no use," said Mr Suhaimi. "The forest top was just too thick for us to signal to them."

The Singapore High Commission's Mr Lim thanked Kluang district police chief Deputy Superintendent Abdul Hamid Haji Mohd Noor for his help.

The hikers were admitted to a

157

its Times

NUARY 6, 1990   50 CENTS MCI (P) 166/12/89

art off
hools

be

s

also aim to be a centre of "community" learning" for residents livin; 'the area.

He said: "Being the only polytechnic in the area, we hope to provide an opportunity for the people living in the area to learn, and can cater to their life-long education. As such, it should be very lively at night, probably with part-time night classes."

The decision to place greater emphasis on technical, vocational and commercial education — and hence a third polytechnic — arose from a review of post-secondary education which the Education Ministry began in October 1988.

This was revealed by Education Minister Dr Tony Tan last year .

He said Singapore would be moving towards an education system in which about 20 per cent of students would study academic subjects and pursue university degrees, and 70 per cent would study polytechnic, technical, and vocational courses.

Missing hikers found

Five show up at loggers' site after their 10-day ordeal

AN OVERJOYED David Hui, 23, hugging his sister Lai Yuet, 29, at the Kluang police station, as the ordeal of Miss Hui and four other missing hikers finally came to an end.

Yesterday afternoon, the five hikers — Miss Hui, two other Singaporeans and two Malaysians — showed up alive and well at a loggers' site, some 40 km south-west of Johor's Gunung Belumut, the mountain they had scaled.

They had been missing for the past 10 days and a massive

■ Diary of the hikers' ordeal.
■ Gunung Belumut safe to climb: Page 19

search was mounted by the Malaysian police. Members of their anxious families kept vigil in Kluang and joined in the hunt.

Mr Lim Chin Leong, the First Secretary of Singapore's High Commission in Kuala Lumpur, who arrived in Kluang early yesterday, told the group that their families in Singapore had been informed of the good news.

"The important thing is you're all safe and unhurt," Mr Lim assured the hikers, who had offered their apologies for causing inconvenience to the Johor police and Singapore authorities. — Picture by AZIZ HUSSIN.

Gorbachev puts off meetings

Singapore thanks our cops

KLUANG, Sat. — The Singapore Government has conveyed its thanks to the Malaysian police for its efforts in the search for five missing hikers at Gunung Belumut here.

The five included three Singaporeans — Norman Shah Kassim, 38, Tan Aik Kee, 28, and his girlfriend Hui Lai Yuet, 29.

First Secretary to the Singapore High Commission in Kuala Lumpur, Mr Lim Chin Leong, who arrived here yesterday was relieved to hear that the five were safe.

They had emerged from the jungle and sought help at a logging camp after being missing since Dec 26.

"We wish to thank the OCPD of Kluang, DSP Abdul Hamid Mohamad Noor for all the help he and his men have rendered in searching for the missing five," he stated.

New Sunday Times 7-1-1990 Page 3.

NANYANG SIANG PAU PAGE 4   6 JANUARY 1990
5 MISSING PERSONS INCLUDING MALES AND FEMALES WERE DELIVERED
FROM THEIR DIFFICULT SITUATION. THEY LOST DIRECTION IN GUNUNG
BERLUMUT. THEY WERE SUBJECTED TO WINDS AND RAINS. THEY ATE
WILD FRUITS.
(KLUANG-5 BY ZHENG YA JIU AND JIAN RUI PIN)

在居銮布鲁木山迷失方向
遭风吹雨淋摘取野果充饥
五失踪男女重见天日

〔居銮曾雅九、简端平五日联合报道〕在居銮布鲁木山迷失方向之五名男女今年元月一时半被送天日，他们恍如隔世，被送到此间警局时，被等热泪夺眶而出，互向亲友拥抱，喜极而谈。

这五名男女是：㈠陈益基（廿八岁），任职於新加坡直落布兰卡一钢铁厂，㈡许丽月（廿大岁），为新加坡飞禽公园园家，㈢诺曼沙卡新（卅八岁），技工，住新加坡式吉巴笃中区，㈣苏海米莫哈欣（廿六岁），技工，以上两人来自居銮加亨甘榜尊多。

他们是於上月十二日上午十时到该山区露营及寻幽探秘。原本订群在圣诞节当天下山，但却在廿六日欲下山却迷失方向，直到今日下午一时许才抵达居銮印打丁宜路十二哩处折入

小路数哩之联邦（马）私人有限公司新多拉区伐木场工人宿舍。

在该宿舍之山大王机及工友们加以援手提供饮食予彼等，然后拨电通知该公司董事经理赖仁宗。赖君获讯后，即从办事处驾着豪华跑车赶往现场，然后将这五名男女载送到居銮警察局。

今日下午四时十五分，赖君之轿车抵居銮警局，车内五名男女一步下车，叫与亲友互相拥抱，彼等悲喜交热泣。亲友们亦高兴得热泪盈眶。

这五名男女皆穿着沾满泥浆、树汁之T恤及短运动裤，手脚皆被野草枯枝刮到伤痕累累，不过精神良好，情绪相当稳定，并接受各报记者、电视台约半小时访问。

陈益基受访时说，他们一行五人是在第五天欲下山时才迷失方向。当时他们所携带之

指南针指着他们之方向是在东北方向，他们知已迷失了方向，即朝西南方而行。他们爬出山坡，涉水而行数日，他们行经过多条沼泽地区及小溪。

他继说，在过去数天来，他们不但饥寒交迫，还遭风吹雨淋，山蜓昆虫之侵咬。夜间他们随地面卧，历尽辛酸苦难。

许丽月受访时说，自迷失方向后，他们便面对无食物问题。为了延续生命，也幸亏大马之两名同伴对野草、野果的认识，於是他们摘取野果如：亚答籽、野香蕉，及类似蛭叶之蕨类植物充饥裹腹，饮溪水，就这样苦捱过今天。

受访时，许小姐也向记者展示他们当日在中充当食物之亚答籽及上述蕨类植物。

她也说，在进入该山区之首六、七天，他们还生火取暖，但在第

八天，他们所携带之火柴皆被淋湿，而在黑暗中摸索。

她继续说，在他们寻出路时，他们曾见到一原住民之废弃空屋及腐烂番薯。在该处他们曾试图制造木筏以便从水路生下流，惟不果。

诺曼沙卡新则对记者说，在过去十四天来，他们不但遭山蚊、山蜓等昆虫之侵咬，还多次见到野兔及熊，当时这些野兽离他们仅廿公尺，他们都很害怕。除此之外，他们也见到无数之大象足迹。

另二名重见天日之本地青年：苏利莫哈末及苏海米哈欣受访时也表示庆幸能重见亲友，并感谢警察、亲友们之协助与关怀。

除了这五名男女之亲朋戚友外，新加坡驻我国最高专员公署一等秘书林振业也出到场整向上述五名男女，他感谢我国政府，特别是警方人员及民众之关怀协助。

这五名男女於下午四时二十分被送往居銮政府医院接受检查。

居銮警区主任何郝哈密副警监促请国外爱好爬山或露营的人士，务若欲到任何山区都必须通知警方或有关当局以防万一。

SIN CHEW JIT POH PAGE 11
7 JANUARY 1990
MASS MEDIA HAS ITS CONTRIBUTION, TOO.
5 TREKKERS FINALLY CAME BACK SAFELY. THE SINGAPORE HIGH
COMMISSION HERE EXPRESSED ITS GRATITUDE.

(K.L.-6)

傳媒也有功勞

五爬山者終脫險歸來
新最高專員署表欣慰

（吉隆坡六日訊）新加坡駐我國最高專員署今日向參與尋找五名爬山露營失踪者工作的我國露警及有關方面的人士致謝。

五名失踪者之中，三人為新加坡公民，另兩人為我國公民，他們是在聖誕節宣告失踪。

新加坡駐我國最高專員署登告訴馬新社說，五人能慶幸歸來以及目前留在居鑾醫院接受觀察，感令人感到欣慰的。

他說：「我要向柔佛州總警長、居鑾警區主任以及馬不停蹄參與搜索工作的人士，致以忠誠的謝意。」

他全時也向大馬大眾傳播媒介致謝。

新加坡政府昨天委派駐馬最高專員署一等秘書林銷龍到居鑾，以慰問有關失踪者。

五名失踪者是於昨日在距離新山約四十公里的哥打丁宜，靠近柔佛中南發展區油棕園一帶出現時，被聯邦火銀（馬）私人有限公司的一名職員發現。這五名人士是前往布魯木山爬山露營後失踪。

當五人的踪跡於下午一時被發現時，健康情況良好。

他們是新加坡的陳益奇，廿八歲，他的女友許麗月，廿九歲，諾爾曼沙敏加沁，卅六歲，以及二名來自加亨甘榜尊多的蘇里莫哈末諾，十九歲及蘇海米哈欣，廿六歲。

他們是在上月廿二日入山，預定於廿五日下山，不過卻迷失方向，直至昨日才走出森林。

160

TONG BAO FRONT PAGE
6 JANUARY 1990
 5 TREKKERS SUCCEEDED IN ESCAPING. THEY ATE WILD FRUITS AND
DRANK WATER FROM THE RIVER. THEY TRIED TO FIND A WAY OUT.
THEY WERE LOST IN THE MOUNTAIN IN KLUANG FOR 14 DAYS.
(KLUANG-5 BY YANG CHENG YAN)

飢吃山果渴飲河水苦尋出路 *TBp81*

居鑾深山迷失14天 *6/1/90*

5登山者成功脫險

本報：楊承炎

（居鑾五日訊）

三名新加坡公民和兩名本地人士迷失在居鑾魯木山瀑布十四天後，今日下午一時半成功自行脫險，走出一樹桐芭伐木場碼頭重見天日，令家屬和各界關懷的人士鬆了一口氣。

這個令五名能在絕望中重生，發現的伐木場是位於居鑾通行哥打丁宜路十二英里處進入的森林芭地哥都拉，離開魯木山瀑布非常遙遠，且方向也不同。

這五名筋疲力盡的迷失者是在今日下午一時半被芭地內龍山大王司機發現，然後引到芭地內的公司屋，公司屋內的工友隨即煮餐款待他們，並讓他們好好休息一會。

五人精神情緒穩定

該芭地的一名書記羅斯蘭同時通知董事經理賴仁宗從阿逸依淡趕到芭地公司屋，于下午四時十五分親自用車載他們到居鑾警局結束整個歷險的過程。

這五名脫險者為陳益基（廿八歲）技術人員，許麗月（廿九歲）飛禽公園管理員和諾爾曼（卅八歲）技術人員。三人皆是新加坡公民。其他兩名是來自居鑾邦命全和加于的巫籍人士。

他們在居鑾警局內外表看來精神還好，情緒也穩定。尚能一一回答各報記者的詢問各項問題，並且在居鑾警局送他們到本坡中央醫院接受健康檢查。

陳益基和許麗月受腳時指出。他們感到很抱歉，這些日子來讓很多人替他們擔憂和勞駕軍警和公眾人士搜尋，在到了最後幾天，他們也作了最壞打算，所幸前能在堅強的毅力下脫險歸來。

陳氏說。他們在第六天便迷失方向，走不回原路下山，而在回程當天他吃白飯而已。第七天隨身所帶的火柴已半濕，不能再生火。接下來的日子只吃深山中的1 河谷果了。喝河水和植物果腹，也遇到是老虎和發現野象的大腳印，不過沒有遇上危險。

發現老虎野象腳印

他說，他們有指南針，五人在迷失方向後便在一條河流上用木料紮一支木伐沿河面下，曾發現一個原住民遺棄的村落和砍伐圓木材的地方，因而增強他們求生的希望。

他說，在他們迷失方向後的第六七天，在天空過聽到飛機聲，過後便沒有聽到。他們在深山中也受到水蛭的侵襲，五人皆穿著短褲，在深山中日與蠟皮尋求出路，形成滿腳傷痕累累。

另一方面，新加坡駐大馬最高專員公署一等秘書林錦朋也在居鑾警局送見三名脫險公民並安慰他們同時感謝居鑾警區主任阿都哈密副局長臨在這些日子來給予各方面的協助和援助，也同時感激軍警人員和公眾人士不辭勞苦的入山搜尋。

UTUSAN MALAYSIA   6 JAN 1990   FRONT PAGE   SHEET 1

THE FIVE WERE ALMOST EATEN BY A TIGER WHILE THEY WERE LOST.
THEY WERE WEAK.

MEREKA DITEMUI TAK BERMAYA

HUI Lai Yuet sedang didakap mesra oleh
saudara lelakinya di Balai Polis Keluang
semalam.

Lagi
gambar
di muka 3

5 hampir dibaham harimau semasa sesat

KELUANG 5 Jan. — Lima orang pendaki yang hilang di hutan lipur, Gunung Belumut sejak 22 Disember lalu hampir-hampir dibaham harimau semasa mereka 'bertarung' selama 10 hari untuk mencari jalan keluar setelah kompas mereka rosak.

Dalam keadaan tidak bermaya dan penuh calar-balar, kelima-lima mereka menemui jalan keluar pada pukul 1 tengah hari ini setelah mengikuti bunyi jentera selama dua hari.

Bila bekalan makanan mereka kehabisan, kumpulan itu memakan buah rotan, pucuk dan umbut kayu.

Menurut Norman Shah, 35, yang bertindak sebagai jurucakap kumpulan itu, enam kali mereka terserempak dengan harimau di mana sekali seekor harimau besar menghampiri mereka hingga jarak 15 kaki.

Oleh
Mansor Othman

Norman, seorang rakyat Singapura, yang ditemui di Hospital Daerah Keluang lewat petang ini berkata, mereka nampak helikopter semasa sedang mengikut bunyi jentera dan melambai - lambaikan tangan tetapi juruterbangnya tidak nampak mereka.

Menurut Norman Shah, mereka mendaki Gunung Belumut pada 22 Disember dan sampai ke kemuncak pada 26 Disember lalu.

"Sewaktu hendak turun dari gunung tersebut, tiba-tiba kompas rosak menyebabkan kami kebingungan dan kehilangan arah," katanya.

Mereka sesat ketika turun dari gunung tersebut dan terpaksa meredah hutan mengikut anak sungai bagi mencari jalan keluar.

LIHAT MUKA 2

SHEET 2

LIMA HAMPIR DIBAHAM HARIMAU SEMASA SESAT

Hujan lebat turun sewaktu mereka berjalan mengikut anak sungai itu dan mereka terpaksa tidur di tepi sungai selama empat malam.

Sewaktu mereka menaiki tanah tinggi selepas meredah payaç separas pinggang selama sehari, mereka telah terdengar bunyi jentera.

Kumpulan berlima itu mengikut bunyi jentera tersebut selama dua hari sebelum menjumpai pekerja-pekerja di satu kawasan pembalakan pada pukul 1 tengah hari ini.

Pekerja-pekerja itu mengubungi majikan mereka, seorang warganegara Singapura, Lai Jn Thong, yang berada di pejabatnya di Syarikat Kilang Papan Federal dekat Lebuh Raya Kota Tinggi, Kluang.

Selepas diberi makan kelima-lima pendaki itu dibentar keluar ke tempat papan itu dan kemudian dihantar ke Balai Polis Kluang oleh Encik Lai bersama Setiausaha Satu Suruhanjaya Tinggi Singapura di Malaysia, yang berada di situ

sejak pagi ini kerana mengikuti operasi mencari.

Kelima-lima pendaki tersebut yang masih dalam keadaan lesu dan calar-balar dibawa ke hospital daerah bagi menjalani pemeriksaan kesihatan. Mereka dibenarkan pulang.

Lima orang yang dilaporkan hilang pada 30 Disember lalu ialah Suri Mohd Nor, 19, dan Suhaimi Hashim, 26, keduanya dari Kampung Contoh, Batu 22 Kahang, Tan Aik Kee, 29, Hui Lai Yuet, 38, dan Norman Shah ketiga-tiganya dari Singapura.

Menurut Norman lagi, semasa sesat di dalam hutan tersebut mereka nampak berbagai benda dan mendengar bunyi-bunyi yang menakutkan.

"Anehnya hanya kami bertiga yang berbanga Melayu sahaja nampak benda-benda yang menakutkan itu," katanya.

Menceritakan detik-detik cemas terserempak dengan harimau, Norman berkata: "Saya yang ketakutan ketika itu membaca ayat-ayat Al-Quran yang saya ingat."

"Apabila harimau tersebut berpusing dan berjalan meninggalkan kami, saya dapati tinggınya kira-kiranya empat kaki dan panjatnya hanya kira-kira dua atau tiga jengkal sahaja daripada tanah."

Menurutnya, mereka juga menemui ular sebesar kira-kira batang kelapa dan tiga kali berjumpa dengan beruang.

Menurut Norman, bekalan makanan mereka habis pada pagi hari keenam mereka sesat di dalam hutan tersebut.

"Kami terpaksa memakan buah rotan, pucuk dan umbut kayu bagi menyambung hidup kami dan menerusikan perja-

lanan mencari jalan keluar," katanya.

Menurutnya, yang mengenalkan kepada mereka makanan yang boleh dimakan di dalam hutan tersebut ialah salah seorang rakan mereka iaitu Suri Mohd Nor, 19, dari Kampung Contoh, Batu 22, Kahang.

Sambil menyifatkan kejadian yang dialaminya sebagai pengalaman dan pengajaran baginya, Norman berkata, dia menganggap Gunung Belumut sebagai lain daripada lain dan tidak boleh dibuat sebarangan kerana sebelum ini beliau belum pernah sesat ketika mendaki beberapa buah gunung.

Adik Norman, Shah Asvan, 28, yang ditemui di hospital tersebut memberitahu, keluarganya akan membuat kenduri kesyukuran kerana Norman telah selamat kembali.

Ayah Suhaimi, Encik Mohd Nor Isnin, 41, dan ibunya Puan Sempurna Jumair, 39, yang menunggu anak mereka di hospital tersebut memberitahu, mereka mendapat tahu anak mereka selamat melalui berita radio pukul 4.30 petang.

Mereka menyifatkan kepulangan anak mereka setelah sesat selama dua minggu di dalam hutan tersebut seolah-olah mati hidup semula.

ENDS

163

CHINA PRESS FRONT PAGE
6 JANUARY 1990
AFTER BEING STRANDED IN THE JUNGLE
FOR 10 DAYS, FIVE PEOPLE INCLUDING
MALES AND FEMALES, WERE OUT OF
DANGER. ONE OF THEM RECITED KOR'AN
VERSES TO CHASE AWAY TIGERS.
(KLUANG-5)

SHEET 1

Singapore

困
森
林
10
天

唸經驅猛虎
五男女脫險

6/1/90 CP181

SHEET 2

CHINA PRESS FRONT PAGE AND PAGE 2
6 JANUARY 1990

（居鑾五日訊）九天前攀登布魯木山而失蹤的四男一女，已於今日下午安然逃出原始森林；其間多次與猛虎、狗熊相遇，幸而其中一人唸起麈歌，才倖倖未受傷害，保住性命。

他們自十二月廿六日即在山上迷路及斷糧，只靠野果、溪水為生，飽受水蛭蚊蟲的叮螫，飢寒交迫，幾乎絕望。

他們翻山越嶺，在森林中與河道間奔闖十天之後，才於今日下午二時三十分到了距居鑾二十英里外哥打打宜大道附近的聯邦火鋸廠工人宿舍。

在逃出生天之前，他們多次遇到老虎與狗熊，相距咫尺，幾乎已活不了，可幸其中一人諾曼沙卡欣略通巫術，唸出可蘭經經文，驅走大虫，才不受傷害。

五人是今日下午四時十分被送抵居鑾警署之後，在精神恍惚中有餘悸地簡略向記者描述逃生經過。

他們抵達警署時，森林區內的搜尋人員還在進行著搜救工作，未完全獲得通知。失蹤者的一些親友還在布魯木山腳警帳等候搜尋消息，未及趕到居鑾市。

陪伴該五人前來警署的是聯邦火鋸廠的六十歲前新加坡轉籃事主席賴仁忠及新加坡駐馬最高專員著一等秘書林錦龍。

（文轉第2版）

（文接封面版）

賴氏說，五個迷路的登山者在下午二時三十分左右抵達樹桐芭裡的工人宿舍。一名山大王司機通知了他，於是他驅車趕入宿舍，安排五人吃飯喝水，才被來居鑾交予警方。

二十九歲的許麗月在警署裡與弟弟見面時，高興得相擁痛哭。三名馬來族同伴也紛紛掉淚，慶幸生還。

二十八歲的陳孟基的兩個弟弟及一名友人，也及時趕到警署會面。能唸經驅獸的三十八歲新加坡技工諾曼沙卡欣說，他們在十二月二十二日入山紮營後，即開始爬山。

於十二月二十五日抵達布魯木山峰並於十二月二十六日下山，不料，半途即迷了路，走向哥打打宜方向去。

諾曼說，十二月二十六日起，他們已斷糧，只剩一罐白米飯。此後十天十夜，所依賴的食物便是山林中的亞答杆（藤果）及山蕨與溪水。

許麗月說，他們曾紮了一個木筏，順流面下，方向是東北，但是，山溪支流交錯，依然找不到路，而且還陷入沼澤裡，慘遭水蛭、蚊虫叮螫，苦不堪言。

她說，他們一遇找生路，一遇丟棄不重要的物件，減輕負擔。搜尋

人員所找到的營帳，便是其中之一。

然而，森林裡入夜之後天寒地凍，他們都儘量留著衣物穿用。

最令他們魂飛魄散的是接連數次看到老虎。

幸而諾曼略通巫術，口中唸出可蘭經文，老虎便乖乖走開。其他四人此後才較定下心來。

他們也見到大象足跡，但未見到大象。

二十八歲的新加坡鋼鐵廠工陳基茂顯得比較鎮定。

不過，在那逃生的最後幾天，他也幾乎絕望。

「我心中唯一所想的就是盡量活著出來。」 6/1/90

再見親人相擁痛哭

半小時記者招待會後，他們即被送往居鑾中央醫院。

諾曼說，逃生到了昨天傍晚，他們終於在寂靜的森林裡聽到重型車桶發出的聲音，於是便朝該方向走，果然最後找到了樹桐伐木場。

新加坡最高專員SR納登，今日表示對三名失蹤在居鑾布魯齊高山十五天後的新加坡人的尋獲感到高興。

他今日傍晚發表文告，感謝柔佛州總警長、居鑾醫院主任及所有參與搜尋行動的有關人士積極展開搜尋工作。

他也感謝大馬大眾傳播媒介，報導整個搜尋工作的進展。

ENDS.

SHIN MIN DAILY NEWS PAGE 32
6 JANUARY 1990
FIVE PEOPLE ,INCLUDING MALES AND FEMALES, WALKED OUT OF THE JUNGLE SAFELY. THEY DRANK WATER FROM THE STREAM AND ATE WILD FRUITS.
(KLUANG-5)

溪水野果樹葉充飢

SM pg 32 6/1/90

五男女安然走出森林

（居鑾五日訊）爬登布魯木山遊玩而失踪近兩週的五名青年男女，今日下午安然走出森林，重見天日。

他們是於下午四時十分，由聯邦火鋸（馬）私人有限公司董事經理賴仁宗專車載到此間警署。

五名失踪者是(一)陳益基（廿八歲），任職新加坡直落不蘭卡一鋼鐵廠，(二)許麗月（廿九歲）是新加坡飛禽公園園藝家，(三)諾曼沙卡欣（卅八歲）技工，住新加坡武吉峇都中區；(四)蘇里崁罕末（十九歲）及(五)蘇海米哈欣（廿六歲）技工，皆來自加亨峇峇。

他們雙腳皆被野草枯枝，割得傷痕纍纍，不過精神良好。

伐木場遇見工友

據賴仁宗表示，五名失踪男女是在伐木場遇見其工友，由其工友將彼等帶回公司宿舍，同時讓他們飽食一餐。

賴氏亦說，他接到工友的通知後，並趕到公司宿舍將這五名男女，載回此間警署，賴氏的伐木場是在居鑾哥打丁宜路十二里處，進芭數里處。

據陳益基追述說，他們登上山頂後，下山五天後便失去方向，當時指南針指示的方向是在東北，於是他們便選擇朝着西南方向行走，連日來，飽受風吹雨淋受盡苦難。

林中見過老虎野象

他說，在第六天時，他們尚有糧食充飢，在第七天後，他們只能以溪水野菓如亞答籽及樹葉果腹。

他又說，在森林中他們的同伴曾遇見老虎，野熊及野象。他因在途中失去他的眼鏡，所以只能聽見老虎及野象吼叫。

他說，他也聽見直昇機的聲音，但離他們的方向很遠。

他對此次的遭遇而引起親友和家屬們的担心，深表歉意，並感謝有關當局。

許麗月喜極而泣

他的女友許麗月神情顯得異常高興，在警署內擁抱着其兄長，喜極而泣。

許麗月說，在他們迷失方向時，他們兩製造木筏以水路下山，但不果，她說，一路上他們也遇見原住民的廢棄物，但屋內的食物已腐壞，他們涉水越嶺飽受山蛭侵咬。

他們較後由警方送往此間醫院接受檢驗。

新加坡駐我國最高專員署一等秘書長林錦龍今日下午也到此間慰問上述五名男女。

Lim Chin Leong

CHAPTER 11

FINAL STINT IN MFA HEADQUARTERS

By the time I returned to Singapore on 23 March 1991, I had about 5 years left to the date of my mandatory retirement as pensioner on 25 June 1996 (coincidentally my birthday!). I was given the position of Assistant Director in charge of Malaysia and Brunei in the Southeast Asia Division. By then MFA HQ had moved to Raffles City Tower due to space constraints in City Hall and expansion of staff. Compared to my previous stint in City Hall, I was delighted to work in Raffles City. There were more helping hands.

By divine providence, I was working with the son of my former teacher Mr P.S.Raman in St Andrew's School. He is Mr Bilahari Kausikan, who was then Director of Southeast Asia Division. We had a good working relationship. Believing in esprit de corps, I was always willing to assist any colleague who needed my help in any difficulty, such as urgent translation, English language usage, mentoring, checking and providing information, preparing a paper for presentation at a closed meeting. Here I recall preparing a paper on UNCLOS (UN Conference on the Law of the Sea)

167

at the instance of Bilahari. I went through the files in our archives in order to prepare a succinct but comprehensive paper. Even though I had never attended UNCLOS, I enjoyed doing research on it. Writing it was not a problem because I had the necessary experience aided by my command of English. When Bilahari told me that the upper echelon was impressed by it, I responded: *"It's also good for you."*

Even now I enjoy research and collection of data, especially on personalities. In fact, I remember a research unit was established in MFA for the first time. I was appointed to head it. Long before that, I was already using my collection of materials from Malaysia.

However, when Permanent Secretary Kishore Mahbubani took over from Perm Sec Peter Chan, Kishore disbanded it for reasons best known to himself. Peter and Kishore are long-standing friends of mine.

Shortly after I had settled down in HQ, divine providence provided the last and final opportunity to meet Sultan Iskandar. I have written something about him in Chapter 10. The occasion was the official visit of PM Goh Chok Tong to Johor Bahru. The entourage comprised Foreign Minister Wong Kan Seng, a few MPs and myself. I recollect meeting Mr Goh for the first time in London. He was then Managing Director of Neptune Orient Lines. After he became PM in November 1990, he paid an official visit to KL where he met PM Mahathir when I was about to relinquish my post. I remember joining him, Mrs Goh, and a couple of his comrades at a private dinner in the hotel where he was staying, because I settled the bill.

When we arrived at the Istana Besar, the Sultan met us. I recall a rather amusing scene where the Sultan was calling repeatedly for his minion Mohd Rahmat, a Johor MP and

Met Menteri Besar in Istana Besar, Johor Bahru, when Mr Lim accompanied Singapore parliamentary delegation in 1986.

Federal Minister of Information. I could not help bursting into a broad smile when I saw him hastily approaching the Sultan with a sheepish grin. I saw PM Goh giving me a wink. Then we were ushered into the audience hall where the Sultan delivered a short speech welcoming us and emphasising the close neighbourliness between Johor and Singapore. Then the Chamberlain showed us the Sultan's private museum. I saw a chamberpot in a bedroom and asked him about it. He revealed that the Sultan's great-grandfather Sultan Abu Bakar married a Chinese woman of Singapore origin.

After the above event, I noticed that only two VIPs visited Singapore, viz. Chief Minister of Melaka Rahim Tamby Chik, Chief Minister of Sarawak Abdul Taib Mahmud. I met the former at our Istana and sat in with PM Goh. Their focal point of discussion was how to promote tourism in Melaka by exploiting its "old world charm". As for Chief Minister Abdul Taib, I accompanied him to meet with DPM Ong Teng Cheong who was asked how to get more Singaporeans to visit Sarawak to enjoy its famous caves and appreciate the culture of Dayaks.

I remember particularly how one bilateral issue in May 1991 between Singapore and the Philippines could spark intense anti-Singapore feelings and hurt diplomatic relations as well as caused investments and tourism to decline sharply. The issue arose from the double murder committed by Flor Contemplacion, a Filipino domestic worker in Singapore. She killed a fellow Filipino domestic worker Della Maga and the 4-year old son of Maga's employer by drowning him in a pail.

One night, while I was on duty monitoring calls, I received an urgent call from a certain General in the Ministry of Defence, telling me anxiously how our Defence Attache in Manila was unable to obtain clearance for our military aircraft to take off and that our Ambassador was reluctant to get himself involved in this military issue. He said he was going to inform the Minister for Defence about this. I told him to give me half an hour to contact the Ambassador. In my conversation with the Ambassador, I urged him to intervene. After hearing my explanation of the consequences, he assured me that he would immediately do the needful and revert to me as quickly as possible. Before the half hour was up, he rang back to tell me the 'good news of the Lord' that clearance had been given and our aircraft had taken off. How amazing that the General rang me up as I was about to convey the Ambassador's message!

The issue of Flor Contemplacion, who was sentenced to death in January 1993 and her execution set for 17 March 1995, involved the intervention of the President of the Philippines, Fidel Ramos, whose two appeals to President Ong Teng Cheong were turned down.

Demonstrations were staged outside the Singapore Embassy and Singapore flags were burnt. Incidentally this is reminiscent of PAS demonstrators in front of our High Commission in KL, where they carried placards "Down with Lee Kuan Yew" and burnt the effigy of PM LKY.

President Ramos even threatened to sever diplomatic ties if the commission he created on 20 March 1995 found Contemplacion to be a victim of injustice. Singapore agreed to re-examine Maga's remains. Prof Chao, our forensic expert, was sent to Manila to conduct the autopsy with his counterpart in Manila. Prior to his departure, he commented to me that Contemplacion was "a strong woman with big strong arms". After a second autopsy by an independent panel was conducted, the Philippine Government finally accepted the original findings of Singapore pathologists.

In stark contrast to Singapore's relations with the Philippines, our bilateral relations with Brunei Darussalam (i.e. Abode of Peace) have consistently been excellent and peaceful. It was by divine providence that I had the opportunity to visit the capital Bandar Seri Begawan as a member of President Wee Kim Wee's entourage in 1991. I recall being impressed by the grandeur of the palace of Sultan Hassanal Bolkiah. As I was walking towards the line-up to be introduced to the Sultan and his Consort (Raja Isteri), the Malaysian High Commissioner Mustaffa Mohammad, who was in a separate line-up for diplomats, approached me and tapped my shoulder. I turned around and was quite astonished to see him. Mustaffa was a Johor MP whom I cultivated a few years before he was appointed by PM Mahathir as a Federal Minister. We had a very brief exchange of pleasantries before the Sultan and his Consort approached us. I was later on ushered into my commodious bedroom. The swimming pool was nearby and as the evening banquet was a few hours away, I availed myself of it. I was surprised to see my Foreign Minister Wong Kan Seng and his Minister of State Lim Hng Kiang already swimming in the pool. I joined them and after a while they emerged from the pool to relax themselves with drinks at the poolside table and chairs. Minister Wong invited me to join them but I responded to let me swim a couple of lengths before joining them. My first close encounter with him was in Terengganu (N-E state in peninsular Malaysia) where he was on an official visit. I did not hesitate to ask him whether he knew my wife Margaret Lim, who remembers him as a technical teacher in Dunearn Secondary School where my wife was teaching. He said: *"Yes, I remember her"* in a friendly manner. I also revealed to him that I was a resident of Bishan where he was my MP. I added that I was glad that something was being done to convert a swampy piece of land into an MRT

President Wee Kim Wee & his entourage state visit to Brunei 6-8 July 1992. Mr Lim was then Asst. Director i/c Malaysia & Brunei, MFA HQ.

Waiting in Istana Edinburgh, Bandar Seri Begawan (Capital of Brunei) during state visit of President Wee Kim Wee, 6-8 July 1992.

Attending Brunei Sultan's Royal Banquet, July 1992.

MEMBER OF PRESIDENT WEE KIM WEE'S DELEGATION TO BRUNEI, 6-8 JULY 1992 (PHOTOS PRESENTED BY MRS TEE TEOW LEE, PA TO FIRST LADY. TAKEN AT ISTANA NURUL IMAN, SULTAN'S PALACE IN BANDAR SERI BEGAWAN.)

Mr Lim in Brunei Sultan's Palace Nurul Iman July 1992.

station near my home. We became familiar thereafter. He was quite au fait with my work in Malaysia. Here I recall a direct experience of working with him in HQ. As I was getting ready to leave for home, I received a phone call from him requesting me to draft something quickly for PM Goh Chok Tong. I did as I was told and brought it to him within half an hour as expected. Fortunately I had a very retentive memory in those days and was always on the qui vive for any phone inquiries from the Permanent Secretary Peter Chan or Deputy Secretary Peter Ho Hak Ean with whom I had a close working relationship. In fact, I was amazed by his astounding memory of my career in his video tribute to me on my 80th birthday. So when I saw a picture of him in the Straits Times receiving the award "Distinguished Service Order" from President Tony Tan Keng Yam on 6 November 2016, I reciprocated in the same manner, especially my memory of him as a kind and helpful colleague. I was not tech-savvy and rather slow in typing. So to help me speed up, he volunteered to type for me. I remember this Latin saying: *"Gratia gratiam parit"* *(Kindness begets kindness).*

President Wee's state visit was a reciprocation of Sultan Hassanal Bolkiah's first state visit to Singapore in 1990 during President Wee's term of office. After the President's return to Singapore, I recollect his lady private secretary requesting me to have lunch with the President at the Istana in order to do a 'postmortem' on his state visit to Brunei. His secretary was kind enough to send me photos that she had taken of me in the Sultan's palace and my memorable river-boat trip as well as a post-lunch group photo with the President at the Istana.

In 1993 I was surprised to be accorded the National Day award of "Pingat Bakti Setia" (PBS). It was a silver cross of loyal service granted to those government officers with at least 25 years' service of "irreproachable character". Prof S.Jayakumar, who succeeded Foreign Minister Wong Kan Seng, presented the award at the MFA Annual Dinner and Dance. Somebody took a photo of me receiving the award on stage and presented it to me later on. It was a big occasion attended by Minister Wong Kan Seng, Parliamentary Secretary Yatiman Yusof who wanted me to give an extempore speech which I declined amidst the loud applause, and other high officials. It was also an occasion for me to have a reunion dinner with my old companions and their wives at the same table. They were attired in exotic costumes. Someone photographed us and presented me with a copy later on. Deputy Secretary Peter Ho made his way to me and offered his congratulation. I introduced my wife to him for the first time.

The Straits Times : Mr Ho receiving the Distinguished Service Order from President Tony Tan Keng Yam on Nov 6, 2016, for his service to the country. As the complexity of the world increases, new tools of governance will be needed. ~ Peter Ho Hak Ean

Mr Lim Chin Leong Receives Award Of
Pingat Bakti Setia (PBS) / Long Service Award
From Minister Of Foreign Affairs Prof. S. Jayakumar
On National Day 1993

In 1994 I was transferred to a newly created division called 'Public Affairs' headed by Ms Tan Lian Choo, an experienced journalist who was recommended to Minister S. Jayakumar. As far as I was concerned, she came across as a friendly and encouraging personality. I remember switching on the TV regularly and reading the newspapers as I used to do in KL, mainly for political and economic news on Malaysia and Indonesia. I recall checking the accuracy of the Malay translation of the English version of the water agreement between Singapore and Malaysia, which was forwarded to me by my former colleague Mr Vanu Gopala Menon of Southeast Asia Division. He is now our High Commissioner in KL.

I also recollect speaking with a BBC journalist calling from London just after office hours. He was pushing for a comment on a sensitive issue. I told him quite frankly that I was in no position to do so. If he desired a statement from MFA, I suggested that he call again the next day and his request would be referred to the appropriate political division. But he never called again!

I also received inquiries and requests from the press secretaries of other ministries. I remember in particular Mr Chan Heng Weng, Press Secretary to PM. He was irked by some of the press reports. I was also instructed by the Secretary to Senior Minister Lee Kuan Yew to convey any request from US notables who wanted to meet with LKY. Apart from all these functions, I also assisted in checking papers for typos and English errors before sending them to the Cabinet. I enjoyed field work rather than these boring occupations. So when the Administration Division circulated 'confidential report' forms to be completed, I asked for a posting abroad on the grounds that my Arabic had fallen into disuse. By the grace of God, I was granted my wish. I was finally posted to Cairo on 15 May 1995.

CHAPTER 12
FIFTH AND LAST POSTING IN CAIRO

After a few briefing sessions in MFA including one with the Mufti of Singapore Syed Isa Semait, I remember being given a farewell lunch by my Director of Public Affairs, Ms Tan Lian Choo with whom I had developed a good rapport through our close working relationship. She was reluctant to lose me and initially she did try to persuade me to reconsider my posting when she read the letter from the Director of Administration.

This time, only my wife and I departed for Cairo as my three children had grown up. My elder son Tien was in the University of Miami, specialising in Architecture while Jit had graduated as a lawyer from the National University of Singapore on a Government Merit Scholarship bond. When my sons were in Raffles Junior College, my daughter Gek, who was with us in KL, completed her General Certificate of Education there. By the grace of God, they were able to live independently. During my brief posting in Cairo, they were able to find time to pay us a visit and do some sightseeing, especially the famous pyramids of Giza and a

Mr Lim exploring the famous Giza Pyramids (1995).

memorable River Nile cruise. They enjoyed Egyptian food, especially the well-cooked soft and tender calamari (squid) and the large delicious 'supreme pizza'. They were impressed by our well-furnished and very spacious apartment. The master bedroom was extremely large. But somehow one old wooden panel fell off from the window and landed on the ground with a loud crash. By divine providence, nobody was around at the rear of the condo where it crashed. Laus Deo semper (Praise the Lord always).

My apartment was within walking distance of our Embassy located at a rather busy road junction. I walked to work until I bought a second-hand Mercedes-Benz. As I was allergic to dust, I had to use a face mask. I was not aware that there were many blood-sucking fleas jumping around, causing itchy swellings and blisters on my feet. As it was quite affordable, I employed a private chauffeur to drive me or my wife who was active in the Asean Ladies' circle. We kept in close touch with our Asean diplomats and their wives. The Asean ladies in particular organised social gatherings from time to time. Moreover, my wife managed to find a Roman Catholic Church in the big city, where we could attend the Sunday Mass. In Chapter 10, I have given my reasons why I declined my posting to Riyadh, capital of Saudi Arabia, which worships the one and only God Allah, and therefore prohibits the establishment of Christian churches in its holy land. In Egypt 92% of the population are Sunni Muslims and 2% are Christians, mainly Coptic. The Copts are native Egyptian Christians. Their medieval language is now used only in the Coptic Church.

For the first time in Egypt, I felt that I was going on a spiritual journey because I discovered several spots pertaining to the escape routes of Joseph, Mary and Jesus. In Heliopolis near the international airport, I entered St Mary's

Church where the infant Jesus was concealed. As I travelled eastwards, I came across a church that was built upon an underground church, where I saw a panel indicating the 'escape routes' of the holy family. I also witnessed some Roman ruins at a remote distance away.

Members of Asean Ladies Circle in Cairo.

After my first exploratory trip, I decided to replace my private chauffeur who was rather jerky in his driving. I managed to find an older, experienced and steady driver. In my second exploratory journey to Sinai Peninsula in the east, we passed by the Suez Canal. Here I must say that the history of Egypt is as fascinating as my journey to Sinai. In 1517 Egypt became part of the Ottoman (Turkish) Empire. Its viceroy Mehemet Ali established a dynasty that lasted until 1953. His successors encouraged the construction of the Suez Canal, but somehow they bankrupted Egypt. The UK, a major creditor, occupied Egypt and established a protectorate. The corrupt regime of King Farouk was toppled in a military coup and a republic was established in 1953.

The radical Gamal Abdel Nasser became President in 1954 and nationalised the Suez Canal in 1956. Nasser was twice defeated by Israel, but his successor President Anwar Sadat made peace with Israel and was ostracised by the Arab world. He was assassinated in 1981 by Islamic fundamentalists and succeeded by President Hosni Mubarak. When I assumed my post in Cairo, he was then the President. One of the things I remember about him was the attempt to assassinate him during his official visit to Ethiopia in 1995. As his car was bullet-proof, he was saved from a sniper's bullet. He was said to have the life of *"a cat that has nine lives"*. This refers to the belief that a cat, because of its natural qualities of speed, cleverness, etc, is very difficult to kill and stays alive in situations that would have caused the death of most other animals. He is still alive, though no longer the President. When I was there from 1995 to 1996, I experienced political stability which he managed to maintain for 18 years by means of the police and military forces. I felt a sense of safety with the ubiquitous presence of the police. However, I also observed hardly anyone respecting the traffic lights.

The desert covers more than 90% of Egypt. The eastern desert, where I was heading, is divided by wadis (Arabic for rocky river beds, dry except during the rains) and ends in the southeast in mountains beside the Red Sea. East of the Suez Canal, the Sinai Peninsula rises to Mount Catherine (Jabal Katrina) at 2642 metres (8668 ft.). As we passed by the Red Sea, it reminded me of Moses, the Hebrew lawgiver and judge who led the Israelites out of Egypt to the promised land of Canaan. On Mount Sinai named Jabal Musa (Mount Moses in Arabic), he received from Jehovah (name of God in Old Testament) the Ten Commandments engraved on tablets of stone. I was inspired to ask my Muslim chauffeur to head straight for Jabal Musa. By the grace of God, we arrived there safely. At the foot of Mount Moses was a very old monastery built like a fort and named after St Catherine of Siena, an Italian mystic of the Dominican order. She was reputed for her holiness and severe asceticism and declared the patron saint of Europe in 1999.

Inside the monastery was a very old church, constructed mainly of wood, which had a library of ancient manuscripts as well as religious icons. While my wife was praying at the altar, divine providence guided me to a side chapel and next to it was a small room where I saw nothing but a green bush. Immediately it came to my mind the "burning bush" that I had read in the Bible where it was mentioned that God spoke to Moses through the burning flames in the bush, ordering Moses, as a result of his fear and hesitation, to go to the pharaoh with his brother Aaron and demand the release of Israelites whom Moses was to lead out of Egypt through the Red Sea. How the obdurate pharaoh was dealt with finally by the Lord God reminds me of the famous proverb: *"God's mill grinds slow but sure"*. That is to say, all the things we do are noticed by God. He will definitely reward those who carry out good deeds and punish those who commit evil, even though the reward or punishment may sometimes be delayed.

As it was getting dark and cold, we decided to pass the night at a nearby hotel. The next morning we rode on camels which took us up Mount Moses, up to a certain spot where we had to dismount. Then we continued climbing towards the summit with breaks along the way. I intended to climb to the spot where Moses was said to have received the Ten Commandments. I saw the sun rays through the clouds around us and imagined what Moses would have experienced at that height. It was a tortuous climb for us, because we could have slipped and hurt ourselves. Being worried about the time it would take us to walk gingerly down the steep slope back to base before sundown, we decided to give the Moses' spot a miss. As I had experienced before, it was more risky descending than ascending the mountain. By divine providence, we reached the base safely. Moreover, our return journey to Cairo was also without mishap.

As a lover of history and culture, I made an effort to visit Alexandria, a northern coastal city of Egypt. It was named after Alexander the Great, who founded many cities named after him. He even named one city after his favourite horse Bucephalus after it died - Bucephala in Iran. His aim was to spread Greek culture and ideas throughout his empire. Some of his cities, like Alexandria in Egypt, have endured to the present day. His successors in Egypt, viz. the Seleucids and the Ptolemies were worshipped as gods. Divine nature was also attributed to their families. All over his empire, Alexander was honoured as a god from whom all his kings claimed descent. No one knows for sure where his body was buried. The Museum in Alexandria had an excellent collection of his sculpture and that of his generals, weapons of war, Greek paraphernalia, pottery, scrolls in papyrus, coins etc. Alexandria was the second largest city in Egypt. I found the inhabitants there very friendly and curious about us, wondering whether we were Chinese, Koreans or Japanese until we told them that we were from Singapore and that I was from the Singapore Embassy in Cairo.

The Egyptian Museum in Cairo was an excellent place for me to gather knowledge of Ancient Egypt, especially its religion. I learnt a lot from the Museum's egyptologist and archaeologist Zahi Hawass. Fortunately Egypt's dry climate had contributed to the preservation of a wealth of monuments: ancient cities, pyramids, temples and artefacts that are a source of wonder today, as they were in antiquity.

Prehistoric Egyptian religion was based on the worship of totemic animals believed to be the ancestors of the clan. Totems later developed into gods, represented with animal heads. Immortality, conferred by the magical rite of mummification, was originally the sole prerogative of the king. They were buried with the Book of the Dead as a guide to reaching the kingdom of Osiris, the god of the underworld.

I recall driving to see the first "Step Pyramid" in Saqqara, which was completely built out of stone during the reign of Pharaoh Djoser (Zoser). Incidentally ancient Egypt was ruled by 30 dynasties of pharaohs from 3100 to 332 BC when Alexander the Great conquered it. Uniquely, the Step Pyramid was surrounded by a recreation of the royal capital of Memphis (southwest of Heliopolis) so that after his death, Pharaoh Djoser would continue to rule his kingdom. The kings of the 4th dynasty built the pyramids at Giza near Cairo. The nearby Sphinx (human head and lion's body in recumbent position) was Pharaoh Akhenaton. Under Akhenaton and his wife Nefertiti, a cultural revolution took place. The traditional gods were replaced by the cult of a single god, represented by the sun disc - the Aten. After his death, Akhenaton was vilified as a heretic and all traces of his rule were obliterated including his new capital Tell-el-Amarna.

To reinforce my egyptology, I went on an organised cruise of the River Nile, all the way to the Aswan Dam and Lake Nasser where I enjoyed spectacular views. I have an album of photos taken of me and my wife, a constant companion, during the course of our extensive travels.

Another thing that I was interested in was the Rosetta Stone that was discovered in 1799 near the town of Rosetta (now named Rashid) at the Nile Delta. It was a slab of basalt with inscriptions from 197 BC. It had the same text in

Greek as in hieroglyphic and demotic scripts and was the key to deciphering other Egyptian inscriptions. I remember two renowned British archaeologists, viz. Flinders Petrie and Howard Carter, who carried out extensive excavations throughout the 19th century. Howard Carter discovered the tomb of Tutankhamen, the only royal tomb with all its treasures intact in the Valley of the Kings at Luxor. He was King of Egypt of the 18th dynasty, son of Akhenaton, who ascended the throne when he was about 10 and ruled for 9 years. He died rather young at the age of 18 or 19. His mother was his father's sister and wife. His consort was his step-sister and cousin, who gave birth to 2 stillborn daughters.

Another fascinating figure was Cleopatra, Queen of Egypt, who ruled from 51 - 48 BC and again in 47 - 30 BC. When Julius Caesar arrived in Egypt, he restored her to the throne from which she had been ousted in favour of her brother Ptolemy Xlll, and Ptolemy was killed. Cleopatra became Caesar's mistress, returned with him to Rome, and gave birth to a son, Caesarion. After Caesar's assassination in 44 BC, she returned to Alexandria and resumed her position as Queen of Egypt. In 41 BC she met Mark Antony and subsequently bore him 3 sons. In 32 BC Rome declared war on Egypt and scored a decisive victory in the naval Battle of Actium, off the west coast of Greece. Cleopatra fled with her 60 ships; Antony abandoned the struggle and followed her. Both he and Cleopatra committed suicide. Cleopatra was Macedonian and the last ruler of the Macedonian dynasty, which ruled Egypt from 323 BC until annexation by Rome in 31 BC. She succeeded her father jointly with her younger brother Ptolemy Xlll, whom she married according to Pharaonic custom.

It was Emperor Augustus who defeated Cleopatra following Antony's liaison with her. (NB: *In ancient Rome, a group of 3 magistrates shared power, forming a 'triumvirate'. The First Triumvirate (60BC) comprised: Caesar, Pompey, Crassus; the Second Triumvirate (43BC): Augustus, Antony, Lepidus. Each was called a 'triumvir'.)*

In 641 AD, the Arabs conquered Egypt, so that the Christianity of later Roman rule was replaced by Islam. Today Egypt is known as the 'Arab Republic of Egypt' (Arabic: Jumhuriyat Misr al-Arabiya).

The Mufti of Singapore Syed Isa Semait was glad to know that I was posted to Cairo, knowing who I was. He briefed me on our students who were studying at El Azhar, Muslim university and mosque in Cairo. Founded in 970 by Jawhar, commander in chief of the army of the Fatimid caliph, the chief Muslim civil and religious leader (from Arabic 'khalifah' meaning successor of Prophet Muhammad). I was to keep in touch with Syed Isa with regard to their welfare and any problems that might arise. By the grace of God, I did not encounter any problem with our Muslim students, who were invited to celebrate Singapore National Day every year. I remember looking after a female Malay Muslim student who was sent by our Ministry of Home Affairs to study Arabic for a year and successfully completed it.

Our Embassy was basically a listening post and covered United Arab Emirates, Jordan and Israel. Where Israel was concerned during my tenure, I still remember the sad event of the assassination in November 1995 of Prime Minister Yitzhak Rabin by a young Jewish extremist named Yigal Amir, who was opposed to the territorial concessions granted to the Palestine Liberation Organisation (PLO) under the Oslo peace accords. With American assistance, he was able to achieve peace with the leader of PLO Yasser Arafat whom I had read and heard a lot in Cairo. By divine providence, I was able to meet him in October 1995 as a member of the Singapore delegation comprising Minister in charge of Muslim Affairs Abdullah Tarmugi, Parliamentary Secretary Yatiman Yusof, Ambassador Rajan, myself and MFA officer as secretary. Arafat came across as a shrewd leader with a smiling face, who welcomed Singapore's offer of technical assistance. Our meeting with him was just after our attendance at the Second MENA Economic Summit held in Amman under the patronage of King Hussein of Jordan from 29-31 October 1995. (MENA stands for Middle East and North Africa.) This was a follow-up to the Israel-Jordan Peace Treaty signed in 1994. I also had the good fortune to be driven to sightsee Petra (Arabic: Wadi Musa). It was a ruined city carved out of the red rock, about 90km south of the Dead Sea. It was captured by the Roman Emperor Trajan in 106 AD and wrecked by the Arabs in the 7th century. I have photos of my visit there. When the Third MENA Economic Summit was held in Cairo in 1996, I was the only Singapore delegate to attend it, because it was all conducted in Arabic.

I had an Egyptian lady translator in our Embassy, who scanned the daily Al Ahram state-owned newspaper on matters of interest to me. I would check her English translation with the Arabic press cuttings before sending them to MFA with my comments. When I first arrived at the Embassy, I examined our collection of books and found the need to build it up with more reference books as was my habit in my previous missions. My predecessor Mr Tan Hung Seng, now Ambassador in Jakarta, did a good job in handing over his duties. I also took over his spacious apartment and his advice to filter the 'potable' water from the tap. Prior to my arrival, he had sent me a useful valedictory report but was a little deficient in that there was no mention of the highly polluted air in the city as well as the prevalent blood-sucking, jumping fleas that caused me to suffer from itchy swellings and blisters. At the end of the day, my leather shoes would be coated with dust and the fleas catching on the lower parts of my trousers.

In early September 1995, I received a most unexpected call from Paris. It was from the private secretary of French TOTAL's chairman informing me that SM Lee Kuan Yew had been invited to attend TOTAL's international advisory committee meeting in Dubai. As I was covering United Arab Emirates (UAE), I told the secretary that I would be there one day ahead of LKY's arrival. I did some research on TOTAL, which was a French transnational oil giant with investments in Singapore. LKY was invited to be a member of its international advisory committee in 1993. He joined because he believed in globalisation and his experience from TOTAL would be of benefit in his role as Senior Adviser to Government of Singapore Investment Corporation (GIC). Its meetings were usually held in September every year in Paris. Its chairman and chief executive was Mr Christophe de Margerie. Therefore it was unusual to hold it in Dubai, which could be considered as exceptional. As far as I was concerned, it was by divine providence that I came into contact with LKY for the fifth and last time. My face was already familiar to him, quite apart from his reading of my political reports, notes of meetings and association with his aides. In Dubai, I recall his trust in me when he personally handed me his heavy laptop when he arrived with Mrs Lee for an important meeting, and asked me to show him the toilet while I waited just outside. I also took notes of the meeting. On the night of his departure, we had a private dinner among ourselves. LKY asked me to join him at the table where he was standing and watching his aides and Mrs Lee joking and delighting in their choice of exotic dishes. Thanking LKY, I said that I had arranged to keep company with his aides at the adjacent table. I added that my Ambassador would be joining him in a minute. He was in a good mood, looking quite relaxed. When it was about time to depart, the aides made their way to the plane first, which was parked rather far away. It was cold outside, besides the unearthly hour of departure. We escorted Mr and Mrs Lee to their car, which was parked at the porch of the restricted area where we stood and waved goodbye to them. They waved back, and that was the last occasion I met them abroad.

There was one case of a Singaporean who was detained for theft in Abu Dhabi, capital of UAE, during the tenure of my predecessor. His family hired a lawyer to get him released, but the case dragged on until I assumed my post. In Tokyo and New Delhi, I succeeded in getting our Singaporeans released fairly quickly. So by telecom I spoke with the lawyer and it seemed to me that it was the police who were dragging their feet and the case was postponed many times. Nevertheless, I urged him to resolve the issue to the best of his ability and hoped to hear from him in a couple of months. Then to my surprise, he finally succeeded in getting the Singaporean released. How amazing! I exclaimed: *"Alhamdulillah!" (God be praised!)*.

Another matter that I wish to recount here was a minute from MFA seeking advice from me with regard to a request for donation from a foreign charity organisation. I made an appointment to see the Director-General of the Religious Department. After an exchange of pleasantries, he asked me whether I knew Arabic. I answered in the affirmative and added that I had studied Classical Arabic for my Cambridge Higher School Certificate. Seeing that I was a Chinese, he was impressed, because Arabic was a difficult language. I revealed that with the aid of some good books which I purchased from Cambridge University, I translated passages from the Holy Quran and compared them with the scholarly versions. I added that I was a teacher then when I learnt Classical Arabic.

Noticing that I was passionate about the language, he presented me a copy of Al Montakhab (The Select) In the Interpretation of the Holy Quran - Arabic -English. The Egyptian Translation, First Translation, Cairo 1993 AD. Published by the Supreme Council for Islamic Affairs Al Azhar. It was indeed a godsend to me. I was surprised to note its publication just 2 years before my arrival in 1995.

After this confab, I showed him MFA's minute. He read it carefully and the organisation mentioned therein seemed to ring a bell. He checked it with his black book and revealed to me that the charity organisation had a link to the Al Qaeda and was merely a front to solicit donations for a dubious purpose. I got what I came for and expressed my gratitude for his invaluable assistance. Thereafter I hurried back to my office and sent an immediate cable to MFA.

Egypt was the first Arab country to recognise our independence. This was due to the friendship of our PM Lee Kuan Yew and President Gamal Abdel Nasser whom I have mentioned above. Singapore established diplomatic relations with Egypt on 28 November 1966. Egypt also sponsored Singapore's membership of the Non-Aligned Movement. So in the early days Egypt gave us political support. Because of this, Singapore is grateful and the relationship of the two countries is on an even keel. Hence, I was not surprised when I was given the role of liaising with the Egyptian GIS. I developed a close and pleasant rapport with the liaison officer who held the rank of a general. After some time I told him that I would like to meet his boss. He replied readily that he would do his best to make an appointment for me. He let on that his boss was very close to President Mubarak whom I have written about in this chapter and was at his beck and call. By divine providence, I managed to have a short meeting with his boss one afternoon. He came across as a tall and genial personality who answered my questions readily. He said that he had been to Singapore and remembered the Orchard Road area. I also inquired of

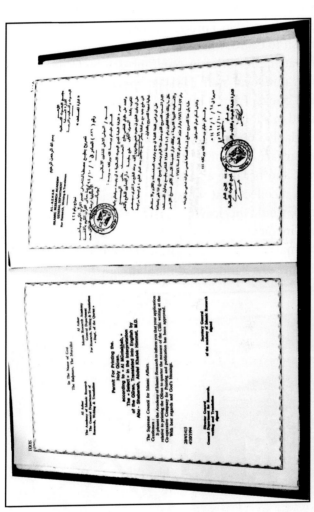

Al Montakhab (The Select) In the Interpretation of the Holy Quran Arabic-English. Published in 1993 by the Supreme Council for Islamic Affairs Al Azhar, Cairo. Present to Mr Lim who has studied Classical Arabic by Director-General of the Religious Dept. in 1995.

him as to the best solution to the Palestinian-Israeli problem. In his view, he was all for a 2-state solution. The problem has yet to be resolved to date. Be that as it may, our relations were strengthened during my tenure in Cairo. This was indicated to me by the powers that be in Singapore. Shortly before I was due to retire in June 1996, Foreign Minister S. Jayakumar made an official visit to Cairo, where he also took the opportunity to take a look at the facilities in our Embassy building as well as chat with our local staff. He also showed interest in our collection of books. I was a little surprised when he beckoned me and asked in a low voice: *"I heard you will be retiring soon."* I answered gladly: *"Yes, sir. I am looking forward to it."* Looking at my familiar face, he smiled. In Chapter 9, I have recounted how we met and became acquainted with each other. Here I also wish to recollect that when the Egyptian liaison officer heard that I would be leaving Cairo soon, he presented a copperplate memento of an ancient august temple. Our kind Asean diplomats also gave me a farewell lunch and presented a silver memento of a handcrafted floral design.

Dinner with Foreign Minister Prof. S. Jayakumar & staff of Singapore Embassy in Cairo during his official visit in April 1996. Mr Lim in red shirt.

Farewell memento from Egyptian liaison officer to Mr Lim (June 1996).

In the months prior to my mandatory retirement, my wife and I made short trips at different intervals to Spain, Lourdes in southwest France, Rome, Istanbul, Crete (Greek Kriti, largest Greek island), Santorini and a cruise around the Aegean Sea between Greece and Turkey. For my wife who is a devotee of holy Mary, a town like Lourdes has religious significance. It has a Christian shrine to St Bernadette, which has a reputation for miraculous cures. There is also a famous statue of holy Mary in a grotto and its spring water is said to have healing properties. Because of this, there are local and foreign people who lie in special baths to get healed. But I was prohibited from taking photos. I also noticed a stream flowing by. When I asked our French driver who was born in Lourdes whether he believed what he saw, his surprising answer was a definite no. It is therefore a matter of faith.

I had a purpose in exploring the Iberian Peninsula and the historical places eastwards to Turkey. I had the desire to understand the rise of Islam through visits to the historic mosques, churches, relics and monuments. In the early 7th century AD, a charismatic figure named Prophet Muhammad united the tribes in the Arabian Peninsula. His religion was Islam meaning 'submission to the will of Allah (God)'. Islam spread rapidly eastwards to Persia and westwards into Spain and North Africa. The Muslim Moors (mixed Arab/Berber race of NW Africa) conquered Spain in 711 AD. After these initial successes, Muslim conquests peaked around 750 AD. Then in the 13th century it won new adherents in Central Asia - the Mongols. Once converted, however, the Mongols took Islam even further afield into India and China. During the 14th and 15th centuries Islam continued to spread to large areas of Africa, and even Southeast Asia (e.g. Malaya and Indonesia). Today it is one of the world's major religions. Islam's initial success was due to a number of factors. Before Prophet Muhammad died in 632 AD, he urged a 'jihad' (holy war) against unbelievers, although the causes of Arab expansion were more complex than a simple crusade. The first targets of this expansion were areas adjacent to Arabia belonging to Byzantine Empire (i.e. Eastern Roman Empire, capital Constantinople or Byzantium) and Persian Empire. These two great powers had exhausted themselves after decades of continuous warfare. Moreover, the Christians of the region belonged to sects that had no love for the Byzantine Empire. In a decade Arab armies conquered Syria, Egypt and Mesopotamia (land between rivers Tigris and Euphrates, site of earliest civilisation). Persia also collapsed. However, Muslim tolerance of Christians and Jews meant many welcomed their rule.

I would like to recount a little on the early caliphs who were successors to Prophet Muhammad. The Umayyad dynasty (651-749) reigning in Syria created a strong, flexible state. However, Islam was split when a combination of dynastic and theological issues produced the breakaway Shiite (or Shia) sect. This consisted of followers of the Prophet's son-in-law Ali, who had been murdered in 661 AD. In 749 regional and Shiite opposition produced a revolution and the establishment of the Abbasid dynasty. The new caliphs removed their power base to a new capital - Baghdad. The Umayyads held on only in their most recent conquest - Spain. Eventually, in 929, the Umayyad ruler of Cordoba took the title of caliph for himself. The political unity of the Muslim world (Dar-al-Islam) was further fractured in the 9th and 10th centuries. The Fatimids (claiming descent from the Prophet's daughter Fatima) established another caliphate in Tunisia. In 969 they conquered Egypt. Once again Shiite forces from the periphery had conquered a centre of Muslim power in Egypt. Meanwhile, within the Baghdad caliphate, real power had fallen into the hands of Turkish commanders. Although the Abbasid dynasty was to survive until 1258, the power of the caliphs was considerably diminished. Thereafter around 1300, the Ottoman Turks emerged as the foremost Muslim power. The Ottoman Empire did much to encourage the spread of Islam. Just as the Christian Spanish and Portuguese spread their religion along the trade routes, so Ottoman venturers carried Islam to Africa and Southeast Asia. Hence its status as a worldwide religion was assured.

CHAPTER 13

MY REFLECTIONS AND BELIEFS AFTER RETIREMENT

The foregoing 12 chapters show evidently that there is such a thing as "divine providence". With the benefit of hindsight, I have written them on the basis of true events in my life. I have no desire to continue working after retirement. By divine providence, in June 1996 Ambassador S.R.Nathan returned from Washington while I returned from Cairo on retirement. He invited me to his home where I met a number of senior civil servants. I recognised all of them except Mr Heng Swee Keat, who was then Director of Higher Education according to the name card he gave me. I was sitting next to him and Mr Peter Ho Hak Ean of Ministry of Foreign Affairs, who knows me very well. Mr Peter Ho told me that there was a vacancy for me in Mindef, but I replied frankly: *"I am not going to work any more."* When Mr Heng heard this, he remarked smilingly: *"I wish I could say that."* Mr Heng is now the Deputy Prime Minister and Minister for Finance.

HC Nathan invited Mr Lim to meet with senior govt. officials from Singapore.

At any rate, Mr Nathan who was then Ambassador-at-Large and Director, Institute of Defence and Strategic Studies, Nanyang Technological University, had primed me of his job offer and asked me to give it a thought. By divine providence, he was elected as President unopposed for 2 terms from 1999 to 2011. He passed away on 22 August 2016. Requiescat in pace (RIP).

Meanwhile, someone who had been liaising with me in Cairo invited me to lunch in the hope that I would join his department. While appreciative of their kind offers, I declined all of them on the grounds that I would like to spend the rest of my days learning medicine and theology.

When friends and strangers asked me why I was interested in those two subjects, I would explain the tremendous need to care for our human body, mind and soul. For example, if I had realised the necessity to have good health till the very end of my life, I would have lived differently.

Good healthy teeth, for instance, are needed till you die. Just imagine the intolerable pain that arises from pure neglect of your teeth. The pain affects your mood and sleep. Then you develop mental stress which eventually causes you to suffer from peptic ulcers and certain forms of eczema. This is all due to our nescience or ignorance. We do not know the psychosomatic nature of our human body. That is why it is necessary to be a lifelong learner so as to be able to treat our body properly.

Theory of Ethics

What is the chief end of human beings? It is to be happy. But we must realise the two different types of happiness, viz. eudaimonism (also spelt eudemonism) and hedonism. Eudaimonism is derived from the Greek word 'eudaimonia' (happiness). A theory of ethics that evaluates actions by their ability to produce personal well-being or happiness. A life controlled by reason is emphasised, rather than the mere pursuit of pleasure as in hedonism (from Greek word 'hedone' meaning pleasure).

Ethics is the study of morals - the belief that influences people's behaviour and attitudes, e.g. work ethic, professional/business/medical ethics. Today, for example, the old ethic of hard work has given way to a new ethic of instant gratification. Here we also need to distinguish between social ethics and Christian ethics. Social ethics deals with issues such as crime, ecology, economics, education, poverty, politics, public policy, racism, war, our obligation to understand, interpret, and reinforce ethical values within a social context.

Christian ethics is the discipline that deals with what is good and bad, with moral duty and obligation. It is a system of right and wrong based on principles drawn from the Bible. The foundation of ethics for the believer is found in Jesus' Sermon on the Mount (Matthew: chapters 5 to 7).

The Sermon contains the Beatitudes (Latin "beatitudo" meaning blessing) in chapter 5:-

> *Blessed are the poor in spirit, for theirs is the kingdom of heaven.*
>
> *Blessed are those who mourn, for they will be comforted.*
>
> *Blessed are the meek (gentle), for they will inherit the earth.*
>
> *Blessed are those who hunger and thirst for righteousness, for they will be filled (satisfied).*
>
> *Blessed are the merciful, for they will receive mercy.*
>
> *Blessed are the pure in heart, for they will see God.*
>
> *Blessed are the peacemakers, for they will be called children of God.*
>
> *Blessed are those who are persecuted for righteousness' sake, for theirs is the kingdom of heaven.*
>
> *Blessed are you when people revile you and persecute you and utter all kinds of evil against you falsely on my account.*

Many in today's diverse theological world argue that everything is relative. Discussions of conflicting ethical choices are seldom rooted in objective ethical norms - rights or wrongs that are right or wrong in every situation. Instead, actions are based on changing human understanding of what would be the most loving thing to do in the situation in which one is found. This 'situation ethics' - an ethical relativism that suggests any action, including murder or adultery, could be righteous in a given situation - is a total denial of Christian ethics. Ultimately, for the Christian, ethics must be based on the absolute nature and character of God. Our "choosing" and "doing" must be based on our understanding of His character as revealed to us in His Word. Bible - Old Testament and New Testament - is the Word of God.

Jesus is the living Word of God (John 1: 1-11).

Doctrine of Balance

For my own purpose, I have developed a mental framework as a practical guide to my own conduct in relation to God and fellow human beings. I call this the "Doctrine of Balance" consisting of 7 deadly sins and 7 cardinal virtues existing in the nature of mankind.

	Deadly Sins	Cardinal Virtues
1	Anger	Justice
2	Pride	Prudence
3	Envy	Temperance
4	Lust	Fortitude
5	Avarice	Faith
6	Gluttony	Hope
7	Sloth	Charity

My comments:

1. To remember the 7 deadly sins, use the acronym: APELAGS.

2. The deadly sins and the cardinal virtues are interlinked. That is to say, we can slide or veer from one side into the other. The left column is for those who will to be

in the "vicious circle", whereas the right column is for those who will to be in the "virtuous circle". God gives us free will. But for those in the vicious circle, they will sooner or later realise that there is a price to pay. I have placed anger first, because it is common and destructive in the end. As for sloth (7), it means the desire to avoid all activity or exertion; laziness. When a person says: *"It is too much trouble to be good"*, he incurs the deadly sin of sloth. Physical laziness is also mortally sinful when it results in harm to others.

3. In the right column, the first 4 virtues are known as "natural virtues", whereas the remaining 3 are "theological virtues" relating to God. A few examples may help you to understand the use of the word "natural" :-

(A) The natural man is not enlightened or communicated by revelation.

(B) Natural religion is belief in the existence of a god without accepting revelation (i.e. Deism). It is the opposite of "Revealed religion" (i.e. Theism). Theism is the belief in the existence of God or a god, especially one revealed supernaturally to humans.

(C) Natural theology is a religion based on reasoned facts rather than revelation. Natural theology is knowledge about God that can be gained by reason from the natural world - apart from special revelation - because the nature of creation reveals something of the nature of the Creator.

4. With regard to the virtue of "prudence" (2), it involves wisdom. The example I often cite is the case of a cyclist at one end of a very narrow bridge while another cyclist is at the other end. Both need to cross the bridge one

at a time. The one who gives in first shows prudence or wisdom because he averts danger or a tragedy.

5. Regarding the virtue of "temperance" (3), it involves self-control or self-restraint without which there will be no sensible control in what you say or do, especially the amount of alcohol you drink. There are others who do not drink alcohol because of their moral or religious belief.

6. As for "fortitude" (4), it is uncomplaining or quiet courage shown in the face of misfortune or adversity.

7. The use of the "Doctrine of Balance" is to enable one to realise the direction or way towards which one is inclined, so that proactive action could be taken to avert trouble or harm.

Categories of Beliefs

We all live by our beliefs. Here I would like to touch on the types of people based on their beliefs.

1. Monotheism. From the Greek "mono" (one) and "theos" (God). The belief that there is one God and only one God. In the Old Testament God strove to teach Israel that He alone was God. The New Testament clearly revealed that God was a Trinity, three-in-one.

    The word "Trinity" never appears in the Bible, though the doctrine clearly does. The Bible states that there is but one God; there are no others. The unity of God is undeniable. Yet this teaching is not inconsistent with the doctrine of the Trinity, which states that there is one essence, yet three persons of the Trinity share this divine essence: God the Father, the First Person of the Trinity; God the Son (Jesus), the Second Person; and God the

Holy Spirit, the Third Person of the Trinity. The three Persons of the Trinity are equal, having only a functional subordination, that is, Jesus was subordinate in function to the Father while on earth. Symbolically, the shamrock is a plant with leaves divided into 3 rounded leaflets to illustrate 3-in-1 concept. Similarly, the same concept may be imagined by means of the hand, i.e. the palm of the hand and the back of the hand are all in one hand.

2. Henotheism. From the Greek "henos" (one) and "theos" (god).

    The worship of one god without asserting that he is the only God and without denying the existence of other gods; the belief that there are many finite gods with one supreme among them. According to Nelson's Dictionary of Christianity, henotheism is a form of faith midway between monotheism and polytheism. It recognises the existence of many gods but regards only one god as the deity of the family or tribe. The Jewish worship of Yahweh (Jehovah, name of God in O.T.) falls into this category of believers.

3. Polytheism. Belief in many different gods or deities. With the exception of Judaism, Christianity and Islam, most of the world's religions are polytheistic, e.g. Hinduism.

4. Agnosticism. From the Greek "agnostikos" (unknowing) or a profession of ignorance. The term was coined by Thomas H.Huxley (English scientist & humanist) in 1869, who used it to show his opposition to those who claimed to have metaphysical explanations of all kinds of philosophical mysteries. It became a prominent banner in the 19th century debate over religious beliefs, and was understood to mean one who held that knowledge of God is impossible, because of the inherent limitations of the human mind.

Robert Flint (Scottish philosopher and theologian, 1838-1910) refuted Huxley's use of the term in his book "Agnosticism", arguing that the ancient term "skepticism" more accurately describes what Huxley believed about God. Flint maintains that Huxley simply wanted to hide his negative religious views.

There have been two types of agnostics throughout history:-

(1) Those who deny that reason can know God and therefore suspend judgement on God's existence (Bertrand Russell 1872-1970, English philosopher & mathematician).

(2) Those who deny that reason can prove or disprove God, but nonetheless continue to believe in such a Being (Immanuel Kant, 1724-1804, German philosopher). This group could be called "religious agnostics".

5. Atheism. From the Greek "atheos" (godless), a word found only once in the New Testament in Ephesians 2:12 - the belief that there is no God. In the 20th century, atheism has grown with the advance of Communism - a political ideology - and the establishment of atheist organisations such as the American Association for the Advancement of Atheism (1925), the League of Militant Atheists (1929), and the Humanist Manifesto I (1933) and A Secular Humanist Declaration (1980).

Atheism has also emerged as a philosophical alternative with the rise of science, challenging the doctrines of Christianity in the 19th and 20th centuries. However, it had already appeared as an alternative Discourse with the weakening of Christianity in Europe during the Enlightenment, which was a philosophical movement originating in 18th C. France, with a belief in reason and human progress, and a questioning of tradition and authority.

Contemporary Islam is also discovering a Discourse towards atheism, which distinguishes Muslims who no longer practise their religion from those who express disbelief in the central truths of the religion. In some Muslim societies, to be branded an atheist would be dangerous or even a criminal offence, if linked to the idea of Apostasy.

Apostasy is the deliberate disavowal of belief in the orthodox tenets of a religion. Not surprisingly Islam and Christianity are the two religions with histories of apostasy and punishments for the offence. The history of the Inquisition and the fact of the sin of apostasy being punishable by death in the Quran are perhaps the two most notorious examples of reactions to declarations of non-belief. However, Islam has generally held that apostasy is only for those who leave the faith and join another.

Here I would like to recount a misconception by pastor Lawrence Khong who was quoted as saying "an atheist is very religious. He has a belief system. He believes there is no God". Mr Paul Tobin, founding president of the Humanist Society (Singapore), calls himself an atheist.

According to him, the prefix "a" in front of "theism" does not mean "the opposite of" or "against". It simply refers to the absence of theism. (See para 3(B) above.) Atheism is not a belief system; it merely describes the absence of belief in god(s). To correct a common misunderstanding of the term "atheism", the Humanist Society (Singapore) was thus formed.

Radical Differences Between Buddhism And Christianity

1. The Buddhistic world view is basically monistic. That is, the existence of a personal creator and Lord is denied. The world operates by natural power and law, not divine command.

2. Buddhism denies the existence of a personal God.

3. Buddhism is a practical approach to life. India had so many Hindu gods that no one could number them. They were often made in the image of men.

4. Buddhism was made in the image of concepts about life and how life should be lived.

5. Buddhism has no God in the Hindu or Christian sense, nor does it have a saviour or a messiah. It has the Buddha who was the "Enlightened One", the Shower of the Way.

6. There are those who deify the Buddha but along with him they worship other gods.

7. The Scriptures make it clear that not only does a personal God exist but also He is to be the only object of worship. (q.v. Isaiah 43:10, 44:6; Exodus 20:2,3; Matthew 4:10; John 10:7-9)

8. There is no such thing in Buddhism as sin against a supreme being. In Christianity sin is ultimately against God, although sinful actions also affect man and his world.

9. Accordingly man needs a saviour to deliver him from his sins. The Bible teaches that Jesus is that Saviour and He offers the gift of salvation to all those who will believe. (q.v. John 1:29; Matthew 1:21; Romans 6:23)

10. According to Buddhist belief, man is worthless, having only temporary existence. In Christianity man is of infinite worth, made in the image of God, and will exist eternally. Man's body is a hindrance to the Buddhist whereas to the Christian, it is an instrument to glorify God. (q.v. Genesis 1:26; 1 Corinthians 6:19)

11. Another problem with Buddhism is the many forms it takes. Consequently, there is a wide variety of belief in the different sects.

    The main divisions are Theravada (or Hinayana) in Southeast Asia, and Mahayana in North Asia; Lamaism in Tibet and Zen in Japan are among the many sects.

My Way of Life

Living in Singapore with a multi-religious and multi-racial society, I adopt "henotheism" as my belief (q.v. Categories of Beliefs para 2 above). Arising from that, I choose to live by the golden mean (Latin: aurea mediocritas). The middle position is the sound one. The doctrine of the mean is frequently the subject of counsel in proverbs, such as the following:-

1. Extremes are dangerous. We should not go too far with our desires and ambitions. We must keep whatever we want within sensible limits. We must not pay too much attention to any one thing, for that might cause us harm.

2. Moderation in all things (q.v. My comment on virtue of "temperance" para 5).

3. Safety lies in the middle course.

4. The best things carried to excess are wrong.

5. Latin proverb: In medio stat virtus. Virtue exists in the middle between two extremes. If courage is the virtue considered, its excess is rashness and its defect cowardice. According to Christian teaching this axiom applies to the moral, not the theological virtues.

Power of Prayer

I believe in the power of prayer. Here I remember vividly my prayer to the family altar in my mother's home in Johor Bahru. My mother was a widow then and I was a teacher with my own family living in Singapore. She lamented the lack of financial support from her 4 sons and 2 daughters who were all married with children. At that point in time, I was doing my course in the teaching of science for lower secondary schools. If I passed, I would earn an extra 2 salary increments. Hence I prayed to the deity in English and asked for help in passing my exams, so that I would be able to give my increments to my mother. My prayer was answered! Now I understand it as divine providence.

At my mother's home, as I raised my 3 joss-sticks to the sky, I would often ask myself 2 questions: *"Who is God? Where can I find Him?"*

Whenever I met my second brother King Sai, we would have an exchange of views on Buddhism and Christianity. However, our knowledge of the two great religions was then rather superficial or even nescient in many respects. He could not answer my questions. In the heat of one exchange, he blurted that I should become a Christian. This set me thinking and I decided to find out more about the life of Jesus Christ. As I read about his life, I began to be fascinated. I was amazed by his miraculous birth, selfless love, his marvellous teachings, divine wisdom, his miracles, immense suffering at the hands of his enemies including the Romans, his crucifixion, death amidst convulsions of nature and resurrection on the third day as foreseen by Jesus Christ. I have never come across such a founder of religion; he is unique. The church worships him as the "only begotten Son of God" who was consubstantial with his heavenly Father, the almighty and eternal God (q.v. Categories of Beliefs: 1 Monotheism on the word Trinity, paras 1 and 2).

My 2 questions that I have often asked myself seem to have been answered by John: chapter 14, where Jesus spoke to his doubting apostles Thomas and Philip. For the benefit of reader, let me cite them:-

"Do not let your hearts be troubled. Believe in God, believe also in me. In my Father's house there are many dwelling places. If it were not so, would I have told you that I go to prepare a place for you? And if I go and prepare a place for you, I will come again and will take you to myself, so that where I am, there you may be also. And you know the way to the place where I am going. Thomas said to him, 'Lord, we do not know where you are going. How can we know the way?' Jesus said to him, 'I am the way, and the truth, and the life. No one comes to the Father except through me. If you know me, you will know my Father also. From now on you do know him and have seen him.' Philip said to him, 'Lord, show us the Father, and we will be satisfied.' Jesus said to him, 'Have I been with you all this time, Philip, and you still do not know me? Whoever has seen me has seen the Father. How can you say, 'Show us the Father' ? Do you not believe that I am in the Father and the Father is in me? The words that I say to you, I do not speak on my own; but the Father who dwells in me does his works. Believe me that I am in the Father and the Father is in me; but if you do not, then believe me because of the works themselves. Very truly, I tell you, the one who believes in me will also do the works that I do and, in fact, will do greater works than these, because I am going to the Father. I will do whatever you ask in my name, so that the Father may be glorified in the Son. If in my name you ask me for anything, I will do it.' "

Application of Wisdom

1. In order to accumulate wisdom, I bought a set of Britannica on "Great Books" of the Western world. I also acquired books on wisdom of the Eastern world including the Quran, the Arabic-English "Al Montakhab" In the interpretation of the Holy Quran by Al Azhar Ministry of Al Awkaf, Arab Republic of Egypt as well as Catholic and Christian Bibles and the ALKITAB (Bible in Indonesian). Additionally I have a collection of religious works and dictionaries in English and Latin for reference.

2. I also gain wisdom from proverbs and quotes from famous men and women in the world. I have displayed some of those on the cabinet of my desk. They are about life and love, optimism and pessimism, fear and courage, failure and success, strength, indomitable will, perseverance, response to change, certitude in divine faith and science. You may find the following quotes thought-provoking.

   (i) Life is really simple, but we insist on making it complicated - Confucius.

   (ii) Very little is needed to make a happy life; it is all within yourself, in your way of thinking - Marcus

215

Aurelius, 121 - 180 AD. Roman Emperor & Stoic philosopher.

(iii) Life is like riding a bicycle. To keep your balance, you must keep moving - Albert Einstein.

(iv) If you can do what you do best, you are further along in life than most people - Leonardo DiCaprio, American actor.

(v) However difficult life may seem, there is always something you can do and succeed at - Stephen Hawking, 1942 -2018. English physicist. Suffered from muscular dystrophy.

(vi) Optimism is the faith that leads to achievement - Helen Keller, 1880 - 1968. First deaf-blind person to earn a BA degree. Ann Sullivan taught her to speak. American author, political activist, lecturer.

(vii) Pessimism leads to weakness; optimism to power - William James, 1842 - 1910. US psychologist & philosopher.

(viii) The optimist sees the rose and not its thorns; the pessimist stares at the thorns, oblivious of the rose - Kahlil Gibran, Lebanese-American writer/poet especially on love. Died in New York.

(ix) Keep love in your heart. A life without it is like a sunless garden when the flowers are dead - Oscar Wilde, 1854-1900. Irish writer.

(x) Where there is love, there is life - Mahatma Gandhi.

(xi) Strength does not come from physical capacity. It comes from an indomitable will - Mahatma Gandhi.

(xii) Life is a flower of which love is the honey - Victor Hugo, 1802-1885. French poet, novelist, dramatist e.g. The Hunchback of Notre Dame; Les Miserables.

(xiii) Good, better, best. Never let it rest. Till your good is better and your better is best - St Jerome, 340-420 AD. Early Christian leader and scholar. He revised Latin edition of New Testament and translated Old Testament into Latin from Hebrew. He settled in Bethlehem.

(xiv) The secret of change is to focus all of your energy, not on fighting the old, but on building the new - Socrates, 469-399 BC. Athenian philosopher, teacher of Plato. Socratic Method vs Sophistry.

(xv) It is not the strongest of the species that survive, nor the most intelligent, but the one most responsive to change - Charles Darwin.

(xvi) It is not the strength of the body that counts, but the strength of the spirit - J.R.R. Tolkien, 1892-1973. English writer of fantasy novels e.g. The Lord of the Rings.

(xvii) Success is not final, failure is not fatal: it is the courage to continue that counts - Winston Churchill.

(xviii) It is not enough to have lived. We should be determined to live for something - Winston Churchill.

(xix) A hero is an ordinary individual who finds the strength to persevere and endure in spite of overwhelming obstacles - Christopher Reeve, "Superman" actor who became paralysed from the neck down following a horse-riding accident in 1995. He founded his Paralysis Foundation in 1998 for research on spinal cord injuries. He died of cardiac arrest in 2004.

(xx) Great works are performed not by strength, but by perseverance - Samuel Johnson, 1709-1784. English lexicographer. Author, critic, brilliant conversationalist.

(xxi) Nothing in life is to be feared; it is only to be understood. Now is the time to understand more so that we may fear less - Marie Curie, 1867-1934. She was a Polish scientist who won Nobel Prizes for Physics & Chemistry. She discovered radioactivity, radium, uranium, polonium with her husband Pierre. She died of radiation.

(xxii) The purpose of human life is to serve and to show compassion and the will to help others - Albert Schweitzer, 1875-1965. French theologian, missionary surgeon, teaching reverence for life. Nobel Peace Prize in 1952. He wrote "The Quest for Historical Jesus" in 1906.

Mother Teresa of Calcutta - Divine Wisdom

3. l also learn divine wisdom from the words of the famous Mother Teresa of Calcutta (now Kolkata), the largest city in India , which was the seat of government of British India (1773 - 1912). She is a contemporary exemplary figure of Christian virtues (cf. Doctrine of Balance on "virtuous circle").

Below is her opinion of people and her magnanimous response:-

"People are often unreasonable and self-centred. Forgive them anyway.

If you are kind, people may accuse you of ulterior motives. Be kind anyway.

If you are honest, people may cheat you. Be honest anyway.

If you find happiness, people may be jealous. Be happy anyway.

The good you do today may be forgotten tomorrow. Do good anyway.

Give the world the best you have and it may never be enough. Give your best anyway.

For you see, in the end, it is between you and God. It was never between you and them anyway."

"Let us meet each other with a smile, for the smile is the beginning of love."

Mother Teresa died on 5 September 1997 at the age of 87. She was canonised by Pope Francis on 4 September 2016. Her tomb is in Kolkata and numerous people of different faiths and nationalities go on a pilgrimage to her shrine. The miracle of a Brazilian man afflicted with tumours, who was cured by her intercession, is well-known. *(NB: Intercession is an act of prayer, petition, or entreaty in favour of another. Some have correctly seen intercessory prayer as one of the most important ministries of a Christian. See Romans 15:30.)*

The Light The Voice And The Universe by V.Siva

4. In January 2003, a close MFA friend called Siva paid me a surprise visit. He used to call me "Mr Chambers" (name of my favourite dictionary) and knew that I had produced a school textbook on English. He needed my help in editing his manuscript.

I gave him my time and free service. He presented me with a large frame of Holy Mary with 14 Stations of the Cross around her. The Stations depict the stages of Christ's journey to Calvary where he was crucified.

Siva revealed that on 20 November 1998, a voice spoke to him while he was meditating and praying to God, without understanding who God was. The Voice said:

> "I am the Supreme God, The Light, The Voice. I gave the Ten Commandments to Moses. I will explain to you about the God you have been searching for and the three worlds which I have created. I am The Supreme God overseeing all the religions in the world, but humanity so far has not been able to understand this universal truth."

After his initial shock, confusion and scepticism, the Voice assured him:

> "So far the world has been experiencing different aspects of Me without knowing that all is Mine. It is time for the world to know that all is one and I want you to write a book to explain this to the world. I will tell you what to write. It is time for the human race to be united as one race and to work together as one family. I will tell you everything about the four dimensions of the Universe which includes the three worlds. You can write about them in simple language so that everyone can understand."

> "I know that most people on Earth do not know or understand who The Supreme God is. Therefore, there are many people going around masquerading as religious leaders with supernatural powers and use My name to rob ignorant and innocent people of their money and wealth. When the truth of The Supreme God and the Universe is told, people would be well equipped to tell the difference between a genuine religious leader with God-given powers and the frauds."

Siva added that "all the various religious denominations diluted the focus on God to such an extent that nobody is now able to focus on who God really is. This was what happened during the lifetime of Lord Jesus Christ who, as Son of God, handled the magnifying glass and focused the teachings of God, The Light, The Voice for the benefit of humanity. The teachings of God were divine truths and properly focused. But over time, many religious teachers claiming to be the chosen ones have moved the magnifying glass out of focus and diluted God's teachings. The Supreme God is very unhappy with this trend and is concerned that with the release of Satan from Hell towards the end of the 20th century, mankind will suffer through the atrocities committed by Satan, if people are not focused on The Supreme God to receive divine help."

Siva said that 20th November 1998 was the beginning of his experience with The Supreme God, The Divine Light, The Voice, which humanity describes as God. The revelations had cleared all his doubts and enabled him to understand God and realise that all religions in the world emanated from one Supreme God, The Light, The Voice. His book captures all the revelations of The Light, The Voice. His book titled "The Light The Voice And The Universe" is available in the National Library. On the cover are frequent questions asked:-

Who is God? What must I do to avoid suffering?

Where do I come from? Is everything in life fated?

Why am I born? What is karma?

Why do I have to suffer? What should I do in life?

I find his chapter 60 on FATE fascinating. He cites the principle of the 75% fate factor and the factor of 25% choices we make in our lives. He uses the analogy of 2 oak seeds.

The first seed that is planted in the wild will eventually grow up to a height of 75 feet over a period of 10 years, while the second nurtured with fertiliser and special care will grow as high as 100 feet in 10 years. He says that our births and rebirths on Earth are fated. These are determined by God. But what we ultimately make of our lives would depend on the 75% fate factor which has been preordained, and the 25% choice factor would depend on the choices we make in our lives. For example, when we reflect back on the events that were turning-points in our lives, we observe from hindsight that, if we had made different career choices earlier in our lives, we could have ended up in different positions in different career paths. The 75% fate factor would ensure that we would have some form of career, but the particular organisation in which we have charted our career paths and the positions we hold now are based on the 25% factor of the choices we have made in our lives.

The 75% factor is also the basis on which predictions of fortune are made. These involve palmistry, horoscopes, physiognomy, psychic premonitions and all other forms of foretelling future events. When an expert palmist reads a person's palm, he can predict the person's future based on what the lines on the person's palm indicate at the time of reading. The palmist would be able to predict with a similar degree of accuracy as one would have been able to predict that the oak seedling would grow to a height of 75 feet in 10 years of normal growth without the use of fertilisers and special care. The prediction of the palmist was based on the 75% fate factor portrayed by the lines on the palm. But the person whose palm was read has the 25% choice factor on his hands, and hence he could influence his fate by the choices he makes. As he makes the choices which influence his fate, the lines on his palm would also change to indicate the direction he is heading.

If the palmist were to examine the palms of the same person 5 years later, he would observe that the lines on the palms would have undergone changes to reflect the changed direction the person's life is heading, as a result of the choices he made during the past 5 years. Similarly, a person's horoscope could predict the future based on the 75% fate factor. These predictions could also be modified by the individual through the choices the person makes with the 25% choice factor. Therefore all forms of predictions could only be at best 75% of what the future would actually turn out to be. All of us can influence and steer the course of our lives with the 25% choice factor. Even predictions of the future by psychics are based on this 75% fate factor.

Another example is the biblical story of Jonah and the Whale. Jonah prophesied on God's directive that He would punish the sinful people of Nineveh by destroying the city and all the people. After hearing the prophecy, the people repented and changed their sinful ways, and therefore God forgave them and spared the city from destruction. The prophecy was in fact a wake-up call to the city. The people heeded the call and used their 25% choice factor to change their sinful ways, whereby God forgave them and altered their fate.

The 75% fate and 25% choice factors could also affect the future of nations and the entire world. Leaders of nations can exercise the 25% choice factor to determine their future as well as collectively decide the future of humanity on Earth.

His book has an Epilogue from which I quote the following:-

"The Supreme God wants the world to know that this book is not intended to create a new religious belief, but to endorse and strengthen all the existing religions in the world which teach man to be good, do good and lead a good life, thus propagating the Supreme God's message, which has been passed down through different celestial beings at various times of human history. The Supreme God wants people to follow the teachings of their own religions and lead good lives."

"The Supreme God also wants to convey the clear message that, while people follow the teachings of their respective religions to reach God, they must realise and accept the divine truth that other people who follow the teachings of their religions can also reach God. The Supreme God has explicitly warned that believers of any religious denomination, who condemn believers of other religious denominations and engage in activities to hurt and harm others in the name of God, will incur the wrath of God and will be punished."

"The Supreme God wants the peoples of the world to be mindful of Satan's release from Hell (q.v. Revelation to John, chapter 20) and change their ways to be good, do good and lead a good life. People should pray to the gods they normally pray to for help in times of difficulties and problems. If you do not have a religion or a particular god to pray to, just focus your mind and pray, without knowing who God is, and I can assure you that God will answer your prayers as

The Supreme God, The Light, The Voice answered my prayer and assigned me to write this book."

"In order to commune with God we need not be a vegetarian; we need not have to perform any form of rituals; and we do not require any other person such as a spiritual or religious leader to intercede on our behalf. Since we are the children of God, we can commune directly with God from any place and under any circumstances. This is a Divine Truth which the Supreme God wants us to know, so that no one can hoodwink and mislead us."

"I have also learned that in this short journey of life on Earth, it is better to die for justice and righteousness than to lead a life of luxury through deceit, treachery and unrighteousness, This truth has been clearly demonstrated to humanity by Lord Jesus Christ who died on the Cross and ascended to Heaven and is now sitting beside God the Father in Heaven."

"A wise man once said: *'I have found my path. You have to find your own path to reach God.'*"

Siva autographed a copy of his book with the following words:-

Dear Chin Leong,

As the chosen "one" you have contributed greatly in accomplishing the task of conveying God's Message to Mankind through this book.

With best wishes
Siva's signature 5 June 2003

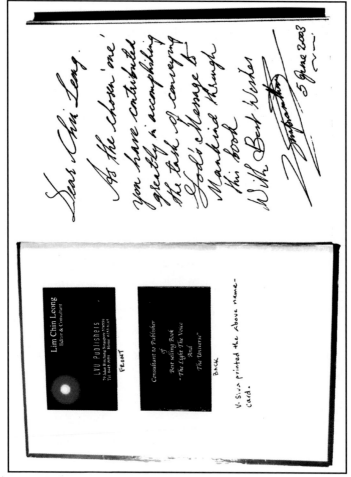

V. Siva's Acknowledgement of Mr Lim's Contribution.

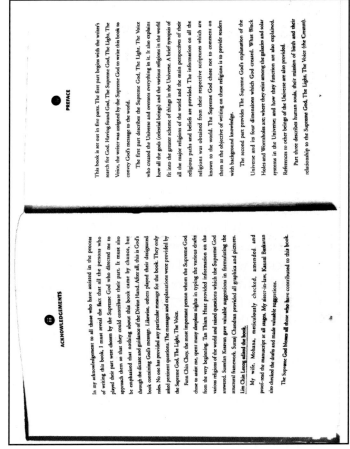

V. Siva's Acknowledgement of Mr Lim's Contribution.

He printed a beautiful name card to show that I am his Editor & Consultant of LVU Publishers. In 2009, he died of leukaemia in 3 days after hospitalisation. Requiescat in pace (RIP).

Leaving Behind A Good Reputation For Posterity

While doing self-study on Chinese, I chanced upon this maxim in 4 Chinese characters 流 芳 白 世 pronounced as liu fang bai shi. The meaning is "leaving behind a good reputation for a hundred generations (i.e. for posterity). I have adopted this maxim as the motto of my life.

As the legendary investor Warren Buffett says: *"It takes 20 years to build a reputation. And 5 minutes to ruin it. If you think about that, you will do things differently."* He values 3 things in a person i.e. intelligence, energy, integrity. The most important quality to him is integrity. If that person has no integrity, he says you can forget about him and do not bother to associate with him. His life advice is the choice of a good spouse. This is where Siva's explanation on fate applies, i.e. 75% fate factor and 25% choice factor. The 75% fate factor explains that the two spouses are fated to meet. Whether their choice of each other is good or bad depends on their 25% choice factor (q.v. chapter 60 on fate in Siva's book).

In the final analysis, as the paterfamilias I must set a good example for my family including my extended families. I must practise the 7 cardinal virtues and be conscious of the baneful or pernicious effects of the 7 deadly sins (q.v. Doctrine of Balance). I do not smoke or drink alcohol, nor do I gamble.

I also remember that a family is a little world created by love. As is commonly known, God is love. The fruit of the

Holy Spirit is love, joy, peace, patience, kindness, goodness, faithfulness, gentleness, self-control (q.v. Galatians 5:22). In Latin, I learnt that "amor gignit amorem" or love begets love. "Omnia vincit Amor et nos cedamus Amori" or Love conquers everything, and let us yield to Love (by Vergil, ancient Roman poet).

I also notice the lack of loving kindness in many dysfunctional families. They do not realise that kindness begets kindness (gratia gratiam parit).l was brought up by my parents and teachers under this regimen or rule: *"Spare the rod and spoil the child."* My headmaster not only caned boys but also girls. No wonder I brought up my children very strictly. The only constant in life is change. Hence we should change as our wisdom grows. As the proverb says: *"Kindness is the noblest weapon to conquer with."*

The family is also the building block of society. However, we should first of all take care of our own family before we help other people, as the proverb says: *"Charity begins at home."* The word "charity" is derived from the Latin "caritas" meaning "love", and it is a cardinal virtue.

As I believe in the power of prayer, I pray for all members of my family including my extended families for their happiness, good health and prosperity. I have an altar in the home where I pray every morning and recite the following:-

"Out of love and reverence for you, Lord Jesus Christ,

I worship God the Father, God the Son and God the Holy Spirit,

One God forever and ever.

May the grace of our Lord Jesus Christ, the love of God and the

Communion of the Holy Spirit be always with us Lord.

I remember you Lord.

I love you Lord with all my heart and soul, with all my mind and strength.

I am eternally grateful for your divine providence or the beneficent

Care of God towards me, my family, my extended families.

I thank you Lord for graciously answering my prayers in times

Of my worry and anxiety over (name the issue).

Facing the frame of Jesus with his aura and rays radiating from his

Heart with the sentence "Jesus I Trust In You" below his feet,

I pray as follows:-

Jesus I trust in you,

For you alone are the Lord who is

My divine light, my saviour, my guide and my help.

NB: The above prayer is the basis of my trust and faith in Jesus.

I learnt from Matthew 7:7 the 3 great divine truths of Jesus, which I have applied in the conduct of my affairs. They are indeed true!

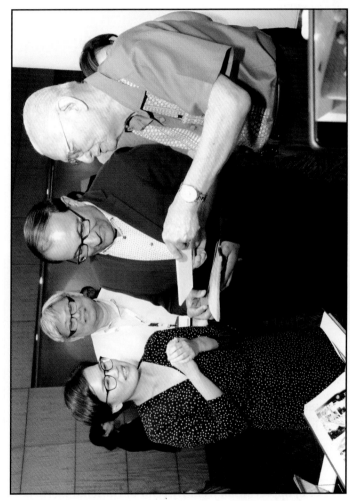

Minister Iswaran shows interest in Mr Lim's rare "Triglot Vocabulary"

National Library Board 100 Victoria Street, #14-01 National Library Building, Singapore 188064   TEL +65 6332 3133   FAX +65 6332 3611   www.nlb.gov.sg

NLB | National Library Board
Singapore

18 June 2019

Mr Lim Chin Leong
Block 6, #15-11
Kitchener Link
Singapore 207227

Dear *Mr Lim*,

The National Library Board and I would like to express our appreciation for the donation of *Triglot Vocabulary : English, Malay, Chinese : Hok-kien, Hak-ka, Character* by Malaya Publishing House, Singapore, 1936 (originally compiled and published in 1891).

This rare title is a useful resource for research on the vernacular languages. It also provides interesting insights to the social history of Singapore through the study of words commonly used by the various communities back then.

We have noted your request to credit the donation as follows:

Donated by Mr Lim Chin Leong

On behalf of the National Library Board, our grateful thanks to you for your generous donation.

Yours sincerely,

Ms Tan Huism
Director, National Library
National Library Board

Letter of appreciation from Director of National Library.
Donated to National Library of Singapore.

ABOUT THE AUTHOR

Five decades ago, it was by divine providence that he was approached by Malaya Publishing House to write a series of English language textbooks. However, as a busy teacher, he was only able to produce one English Language textbook entitled "A Book of Comprehension, Precis and Composition Exercises" based on his professional skill in the teaching of English as a second language. It was recommended by the Singapore Ministry of Education to be used in English Secondary Schools and Vernacular Secondary Schools. It went through several reprints even as the author was seconded to the Ministry of Foreign Affairs. The textbook was so popular that it even attracted a fair amount of piracy in Singapore and across the border.

This latest masterpiece, an autobiography which is his magnum opus, was written with the inspiration of divine providence. Also by divine providence, he has produced a third bilingual English-Chinese learning book: "Learn English Through Chinese". It is in the process of being published and intended for the Chinese market.

The author is an octogenarian who wishes to spend the rest of his days writing for the good of humanity.